The Bible:

Fact or Fiction?

by

Dr. Robert G. Witty

CLC ❖ PUBLICATIONS

Fort Washington, Pennsylvania 19034

Published by CLC ❖ Publications

U.S.A.
P.O. Box 1449, Fort Washington, PA 19034

GREAT BRITAIN
51 The Dean, Alresford, Hants. SO24 9BJ

AUSTRALIA
P.O. Box 419M, Manunda, QLD 4879

NEW ZEALAND
10 MacArthur Street, Feilding

ISBN 0-87508-638-1

This printing 2001

• • • • •

In Part One, the Scripture quotations are all from the New International Version (NIV), copyrighted © 1973, 1978, 1984 by International Bible Society.

In Part Two, a compilation from many authors, the versions vary in accordance with the original source and may or may not be indicated.

Scripture quotations identified KJV are from the King James Version of the Bible.

Scripture quotations identified NKJV are from the New King James Version of the Bible, copyrighted © 1979, 1980, 1982 by Thomas Nelson, Inc.

Scripture quotations identified NASB are from the New American Standard Bible, copyrighted © 1960, 1971, 1977, 1995 by The Lockman Foundation.

CONTENTS

Part One: Examining the Evidence

Part Two: Evidence Confirmed

THE BIBLE:
Fact or Fiction?

Preface

I believe in the validity of the Bible.

All my adult life a vague concern about the validity of the Bible as the Word of God has nagged me. I reasoned: Why would a wise and compassionate God not provide the common man with a simple, tangible, and common-sense proof of the validity of the Biblical record? Surely our Heavenly Father would not have limited spiritual certainty about the truth of the Bible to only the scholar, the philosopher and the theologian. This conviction has led me in a quest that any intellectually honest person can follow. My procedure is meant to be simple rather than scholarly. My search for an answer reaches out to common sense, logic, and fair judgment rather than to academics.

R. A. Torrey, whose reputation as a Bible scholar has bridged more than one generation, emphasized his own personal conviction about the common man's ability to understand the Bible. Torrey declared, "I am always suspicious of profound explanations of the Scriptures, explanations that require a scholar or philosopher to understand them. The Bible is a plain man's book. The Lord Jesus himself said in Matthew 11:25, 'I thank thee, O Father, Lord of heaven and earth, that thou didst hide those things from the wise and understanding, and didst reveal them unto babes.' In at least ninety-nine cases in a hundred the meaning of Scripture that lies on the surface, the meaning that any simple-minded man, woman, or child who really wants to know the truth and to obey it would see in it, is what it really means." What Torrey wrote was a great encouragement to my belief that a loving God would provide a common man's proof of the validity of His Word. Of course, I also realized that only those who are willing to make an unprejudiced judgment could reach the correct answer.

Having read Torrey's statement, you should not think me presumptuous to propose that a compassionate God has established a method by which the Bible is able to prove its own validity to the ordinary reader.

I venture to claim, therefore, that this book explains this available but often ignored proof: God's gracious provision for the ordinary but sincere person who really wants to know the truth about the Bible.

What you will read in this book is in no way meant to lessen the Christian believer's personal testimony of salvation as a proof for the validity of the Bible. What a wonderful gift is the inward assurance our Heavenly Father gives to each of His children! Romans 8:16 says it best: *"The Spirit himself testifies with our spirit that we are God's children."* Nor is this book intended to disparage Christian scholars' contributions based upon logical reasoning and scientific investigation. Devout scholars have exploded much, though obviously not all, of the skeptics' cavil against the Bible as the ultimate authority for the Christian's faith. Thank God for Christian scholars!

I agree that both the believer's inward assurance and the scholar's logical reasoning make unique and valued contributions to human need for spiritual certainty. Both of these evidences afford sources of spiritual strength, but only for those who willingly accept their validity.

This book rests its claim for a solid proof of the validity of the Bible upon a single tangible and undeniable fact: We have a book that we call the BIBLE. Anyone can see and handle this book. The Bible IS!

The Bible is a tangible fact! Admittedly, different people assign a variety of values to the Bible. Some accept the Bible as inerrant truth. Others hold that the Bible mixes truth with error. Still others reject all claims of special inspiration for the Bible. But all must accept one undeniable fact: We do have a book called the Bible.

I repeat for emphasis: The evidence for the validity of the Bible that is presented in this book rests upon this one simple, tangible, and undeniable fact: the Bible IS! This one single fact can provide any open-minded person with tangible proof for the validity of the Bible and for what it teaches.

I believe that the Bible itself, given the opportunity, proves its own validity beyond any reasonable doubt.

*To Pat Hoover—faithful daughter, mother,
wife, & Christian witness.*

CHAPTER ONE

The Inward Personal Assurance

One Christian said, "If you wish, I will tell you how I know the Bible is true."

"Please do," I replied.

"The Bible teaches that if a sinner will repent of his sins and believe on the Lord Jesus Christ, God will save him. I did exactly what the Bible taught and God forgave me of my sins. Such a change in my life must be real and from God. I put the Bible to the test and my personal experience has proved that the Bible is true."

Without denying the value of this personal testimony, fair judgment requires an admission of weakness in this method of attempting to prove the validity of the Bible. Though the believer claims that personal experience is strong evidence for Bible validity, the skeptic considers such proof to be weak and entirely subjective.

Though such inward assurance possesses no external or tangible evidential support, it needs none for the believer. Faith has grasped spiritual reality and experienced God's confirming inward response. Though this inward faith does manifest itself in the believer's outward lifestyle, the assurance remains inward to the believer. The personal and inward witness is incapable of any external or tangible proof of its own validity to the skeptical unbeliever. Such assurance is the believer's personal treasure but no proof to the skeptic.

The Apostle Paul was referring only to his own inward assurance when he wrote to Timothy, *I know whom I have believed.*

The Apostle Simon Peter was rejoicing only in this inward assurance of Christian believers when he wrote of their personal relation to Christ, *Though you have not seen him, you love him, and even though you do not see him now, you believe in him and are filled with inexpressible and glorious joy.*

In fact, Jesus was commending only this inward personal assurance when he said to Thomas, "... *blessed are those who have not seen and yet have believed.*"

What the Bible teaches about the limited benefits of the evidence of personal assurance of salvation has found abundant confirmation in Christian biography. Though Saint Augustine, Bishop of Hippo Regius, continues to receive lasting recognition as a philosopher and theologian, the young Augustine could give no tangible or objective proof of the reality of the Voice which had instructed him to read and heed Paul's admonition: *Clothe yourselves with the Lord Jesus Christ, and do not think about how to gratify the desires of your sinful nature.* The Voice was real only to Augustine. Though what he experienced in Milan transformed his life and subsequent ministry, the reality of the experience was personal, spiritual, subjective, intangible.

The Reverend John Wesley—at one time a legalistic and ineffective missionary to the Indians living in Georgia—had no objective evidence or tangible substantiation when he later testified to his inward heartwarming experience at the Aldersgate mission in London on May 24, 1738. Though what he experienced transformed his continuing ministry and in due time gave birth to Methodism, the reality of the experience was personal, spiritual, intangible.

Though the Christian's inward personal assurance of spiritual reality defies laboratory analysis and lacks objective and tangible vindication, the believer requires no additional proof because "he knows that he knows."

Admittedly, this inward and personal spiritual experience has both strengths and weaknesses. Two strengths of the personal inward assurance deserve special mention: *one*, comfort to the believer and, *two*, contagion to some unbelievers.

Lidie H. Edmunds expressed the comfort of inward assurance to the believing person in a poem: "My faith has found a resting place—not in device nor creed; I trust the Everliving One, . . . I need no other argument, I need no other plea. . . ."

John Newton, author of *Amazing Grace*, testified to this same comfort in his personal experience with Jesus, saying, "Dear name!

the Rock on which I build, my Shield and Hiding Place."

Indeed, millions have professed that this inward and very personal assurance has produced peace and joy in living, strength and assistance in sorrow, guidance in decisions, certainty of hope in sickness and death. No other assurance has borne such precious fruit. No other personal conviction has clothed daily living with service to others; no other belief arrays inescapable dying with visions of eternal glory. Christians continue to testify that God-given inward assurance confers the strength of satisfying personal spiritual comfort.

A second strength grows out of the unique power of the Christian's testimony of inward assurance of personal salvation, persuading some unbelievers to seek and receive their own faith relationship. Shared personal assurance becomes contagious. The book of Acts records six opportunities for Paul to speak before unbelievers. In each case the learned Apostle chose to share his personal inward experience rather than to attempt academic proof for his new faith. Paul relied upon the unique power of the shared testimony of inward assurance to convince and to persuade others.

When I was a small boy in Glasgow, Kentucky, I heard the testimonies of assurance of salvation given by a group of adults in the general assembly of our Sunday School. Though I can recall no specific statement made by these laypersons, I have never escaped that early conviction that what I heard was genuine. The fellowship with God through Jesus Christ and the resulting peace and hope that they professed as personal experiences became the experience I craved!

The amazing contagion of Campus Crusade affords a contemporary record of the worldwide power of shared inward assurance to stir conviction and create desire in the hearer. Not the force of tangible evidences but the earnest sincerity of shared inward assurance has inspired millions to replace unbelief with faith. These new believers have confessed that their new-found faith has given them the same personal and inward assurance they had heard in others.

How does the Bible explain the transforming power of this

communicated inward assurance? Scripture teaches that in addition
to the zeal, earnestness, and sincerity of the human witness, the
Holy Spirit uses this sharing of personal experience to produce a
God-given conviction and spiritual yearning in unsaved persons.
Consider how the first believers evangelized and what words they
used in reaching unbelievers: *Day after day, in the temple courts
and from house to house, they never stopped teaching and
proclaiming the good news that Jesus is the Christ* (Acts 5:42). In
fact, was not this Jesus' plan?: ". . . *and you will be my witnesses in
Jerusalem, and in all Judea and Samaria, and to the ends of the
earth*" (Acts 1:8).

Personal subjective witness was not used to prove the validity
of the Bible but for evangelizing the lost. Then as well as now,
personal testimony to inward assurance suffers a certain weakness:
No matter how earnestly the believer may share what he has
experienced, the skeptical hearer may simply reject its reality.
Personal witness possesses no tangible or objective evidence apart
from the believer's word—no ability to refute the frequent rejection.

Continuing study and varied experience may reveal other
strengths and weaknesses to the believer's possession and sharing
of inner personal assurance. The strengths have sounded forth a
strong challenge for Christians to share their personal and inward
assurance with others. Even the weaknesses evident in this personal
assurance lack the ability to silence the obedient Christian's witness,
motivated by the love of Christ for the unbeliever. Certainly, nothing
in this book must belittle the value or the power of God's gracious
gift of inward assurance to the believer. How amazing that the simple
sharing of personal inward assurance has already comforted millions
of Christians and convinced vast numbers of sincere inquirers!

Yet a weakness remains: the believer's personal testimony of
assurance of salvation has no external or tangible proof for the
skeptic. When the Christian has given his sincerest witness, the
unbeliever can reply, "Though I admit the sincerity of your testimony
and changed life, my logical judgment cannot agree with your
spiritual conclusion that this salvation is necessary, logical, or correct.
No doubt your professed inward assurance may satisfy you, but I

see no tangible or objective proof of its validity that merits my belief. The fact that you, as a believer, claim an inward assurance of salvation by obeying the Bible formula fails to afford me with any credible proof that the Bible is true. I would explain your testimony of assurance on the basis of psychology."

The personal testimony—a gift from God whose value cannot be estimated—remains a claim based only on a subjective experience. What the Christian can declare, the skeptic can deny or attribute to a natural cause. And if what the Christian testifies about the deity source of his salvation falls short of proving its reality to the skeptic, then any Christian's claim about the validity of the Bible based upon a subjective experience will likewise fall short of objective proof to the skeptic.

The evidence for the validity of the Bible that we will soon be considering differs from this God-given inward assurance, for the book we call the Bible is an external, tangible, and objective fact.

The Bible is a tangible object containing records which cannot be denied without proof. For this reason, the evidence that will be presented here, which is based solely on the book known as the Bible, requires an adequate explanation for the Bible's contents—and it remains for the skeptic to refute its validity.

CHAPTER TWO

The Scholar's Arguments

For the Christian to be fair, he must also admit that scholarly arguments to prove the existence of God do not prove the validity of the Bible. If the Bible is proved to be true, then the existence of God is true; on the other hand, proving that God exists does not prove that the Bible is true. The fact that God exists is a separate matter from the truth that the Bible is the Word of God. A few examples will demonstrate both the theological strength of these arguments for God and their failure to prove the validity of the Bible.

Despite his contrary theological views, the agnostic Robert G. Ingersoll is said to have accepted a personal invitation to view a gift received by his pastor friend Phillips Brooks. The gift, a scale model of the nearby universe, fascinated Ingersoll as he watched the coordinated mechanism replicating the movement of the bodies of our solar system.

"What an amazing machine," marveled the famous agnostic. "Who made it for you?"

"No one," laughed the minister. "The device came together just as you claim our universe originated. The entire system just came together by accidental chance!"

Whether true or fictitious, the story illustrates how the human mind can react to scholarly arguments concerning the Bible, the reality of God, and the spirit world. For example, in spite of all the evidences for creation, belief in evolution by random chance has displaced God as Creator in the minds of many unbelievers. Belief in the validity of the Bible suffers a similar rejection.

Godly scholars have attempted to remove doubt about the fact and the work of God with logical reasoning and scientific investigations. Some people can and do confirm their faith in the existence of God by accepting the scholar's logical reasoning and the scientific evidences. Others simply reject the unwanted spiritual arguments as inconclusive or incorrect. But this story illustrates the fact that scholarly arguments and analogies are not final proof of any spiritual reality to the unbeliever.

Scholarly arguments to prove the existence of God may be divided into two segments: logical apologetics and scientific evidences. However, in some presentations the two segments unite.

Logical Apologetics

Logical apologetics are reasons for accepting the existence of God. Scholars developed theological, intellectual, and reasonable proofs of God over several centuries before the contemporary emphasis upon the so-called scientific method. Textbooks usually divide these intellectual arguments for God's existence and power as follows: the cosmological, the teleological, the anthropological, and the ontological. Each argument has strength but also weakness in its effort to prove that God exists. Here is a summary of the four arguments presented in as simple a form as possible. Without denying their unique value as logical arguments for the existence of God, honesty requires the admission that they fail to prove the validity of the Bible.

First, consider the *cosmological argument*: the universe demands an adequate external cause. This scholarly argument, like the law that every effect requires an adequate cause, rests on the assumption that the physical world must have had an origin, a "beginning." The strength of the argument lies in the assumption that the cosmic "beginning" must have a producing cause. The Bible certainly agrees that "the things that are made" show two facts: the eternal power and Godhead of the Creator. The weakness of the cosmological argument lies both in the materialist's contention that matter is eternal and in the believer's admission that the material cosmos fails to reveal essential attributes of the God of the Bible, such as holiness, mercy, and grace. Though the cosmological argument makes belief in deity reasonable to those who accept its reasoning, it admittedly falls short of proving the validity of the Bible.

Secondly, consider the *teleological argument*. This scholarly argument, basically that cosmic design requires an adequate designer, rests on the fact that "order" and "collocating" are universally present in our universe and, therefore, require an adequate and "orderly" intelligence in the designer. The Bible agrees with this fact in God's answer to Job about the order in God's creation (Job 38). The weakness of the teleological argument lies both in the evolutionist's contention for widespread natural selection and in the believer's admission that the design fails to reveal essential attributes of the God of the Bible such as holiness, mercy, and grace. Though the teleological argument makes belief in God reasonable to those who accept its reasoning, it admittedly falls short of proving the validity of the Bible.

Thirdly, consider the *anthropological argument*. This scholarly argument goes beyond both the cosmological and the teleological arguments by claiming that the causative power must possess the necessary factors of personality that are required in order to produce the human being. How is this done? The greatest strength of this argument is the claim that the human, who must have had a "beginning," requires a producing cause that is sufficient to account for his reasoning ability, his self-consciousness, and his moral nature. While this argument comes closer to requiring the God of the Bible, it fails to prove God's attributes of holiness or redemptive grace. Moreover, the evolutionist claims that natural processes can account for all human abilities. Though the anthropological argument makes belief in God reasonable to those who accept its reasoning, it admittedly falls short of proving the validity of the Bible.

Fourthly, consider the *ontological argument*. This scholarly argument stands on the logical inference that only the actual existence of God can account for the presence of abstract and necessary ideas in the human mind. Three forms of this argument have received special recognition.

1. Samuel Clarke contended that time and space are necessary attributes of substance or being. If time and space are infinite and eternal, he contended that this assumption requires an infinite and eternal substance or being to whom these attributes belong.

2. Descartes contended that man innately has the idea of an

infinite and perfect being. Believing that imperfect and finite beings could not produce this idea of infinite perfection unless the idea represented reality, he therefore asserted that the innate ideas require the actual existence of an infinite and perfect cause.

3. Anselm contended that actual existence is a necessary attribute of perfection; therefore, he claimed that the fact that man has a concept of perfection requires the existence of a perfect being.

The greatest weakness of the ontological argument lies in the fact that it rests upon what is actually only an assumption. The skeptic needs only to express his disagreement. There is no tangible or external evidence to prove the argument's validity. Great scholars like the above may have proved that belief in God is intellectually reasonable—and this is a valuable service. But it admittedly falls short of proving the validity of the Bible.

These four historic intellectual arguments—the cosmological, the teleological, the anthropological, and the ontological—deserve recognition because they afford logical support to a reasonable acceptance of belief in God. Even the believer must admit, however, that they still fail to require the essential attributes of the God of the Bible. And the materialist, though admiring the logic, can simply deny the assumptions and assign the conclusions to evolutionary processes. Despite their forensic value, honesty requires the admission that these historic arguments of the scholars fall short of proving the validity of the Bible.

Physical and Scientific Evidences

The Reverend Joseph Butler, Bishop of Durham, England, published his famous *Analogy of Religion* in 1736. Without robbing this classic of just praise for presenting analogies between nature and spiritual truth, even Butler's admirers have confessed that his work does not refute the materialist or the evolutionist. The physical and material must ever lack the power to reveal the fullness of the eternal and the spiritual. Nature's analogies can indicate the presence and the handiwork of God to the believer but will always fall short of revealing the full nature of God's holy and gracious character. In fact, only the eye of faith sees proof in nature of the existence of God. Television programs about nature illustrate both the power and the weakness of the wonders of the physical realm to prove or even to indicate the presence or work of deity. When the believer considers the immensity of space, the majesties of earth, the amazing life forms of land and sea, he rejoices, "How great and wonderful are the works of God!" When the unbeliever sees the same natural phenomena, he declares, "How intricate and remarkable are the adaptations of evolution."

Both the Psalmist and the great Apostle Paul could claim only that the material creation gives proof of the presence and power of God, and that only to a person having faith. What man experiences by his reasoning or by his five senses fails to reveal the full glory of the holy nature of the God of the Bible. Paul admits that "in the wisdom of God the world by wisdom knew not God. . . ." Logical reasoning and scientific investigation will always fall short of demonstrating the holiness and grace of God.

The "bottom line" can claim only that scholarly and logical arguments and scientific investigations have made faith in God intellectually reasonable; they can go no further. The believer must admit that man's best arguments and discoveries fall short of revealing the holy and gracious nature of the God of the Bible. And the confirmed unbeliever may retain his unbelief because intellectual arguments and scientific evidences only confirm what faith already believes. Without Christian faith, the materialist explains nature's wonders by the evolutionary processes. It is certain, therefore, that the scholarly arguments and scientific evidences which fall short of proving the reality of God fail completely in proving the validity of the Bible.

The evidences presented in this book are meant to detract no honor from the inward spiritual response that God gives to each believer in response to his faith. God's assurance may give adequate proof about the validity of the Bible to the true believer, yet the unbeliever can defend his rejection on the ground of lack of objective and tangible evidence.

In the previous chapter we frankly admitted the failure of sincere affirmations based on the personal and subjective experience of the believer to validate the Bible. What you have read in this chapter makes the additional admission that the logical evidences produced by scholars who confirm faith with reason fall short also of validating the Bible. Christian scholarship and increasing knowledge of our universe may strengthen the faith of the believer, but the unbeliever can refuse the arguments and even defend his rejection on the ground of natural and materialistic processes.

The objective evidence for the validity of the Bible that will be presented in the remaining chapters will differ from scholarly reasoning and intellectual subjective arguments.

The Bible IS! The Bible has actual, objective, tangible, factual contents. The validity of the Bible deserves a fair appraisal based on an adequate and reasonable explanation of the source and significance of its contents. The following chapters attempt to provide that fair judgment and a reasonable conclusion concerning the validity of the Bible based upon an adequate explanation of its contents.

CHAPTER THREE

The Basis for Fair Judgment of the Bible

The fact that you are continuing to read this book is an indication that you wish to make a fair and unprejudiced appraisal of this important question concerning the validity of the Bible.

We readily admit that a believer's inward assurance cannot prove the validity of the Bible to the unbeliever. We also admit that the scholar's reasoning and scientific evidences cannot prove the validity of the Bible. On what reasonable grounds, therefore, do I claim that just the Book itself—the contents of the Bible—offers such complete evidence of its own validity that this single proof is beyond reasonable rebuttal? The grounds that establish a reasonable basis of proof are twofold: fairness and facts.

The first necessary basis: *Judge the Bible with fairness*.

Fair judgment never rests upon prejudgment, and most especially upon prejudice that is based upon personal ignorance or upon uncritical acceptance of the biased conclusions of other people. When these secondhand critics are challenged, their inability to substantiate their conclusions with specific examples reveals their lack of factual evidence. In fact, even some firsthand critics have never read the complete text of the Bible, nor have they examined the scholarly Biblical defenses. Such judgment is unfair and prejudiced.

Fair judgment never rests upon philosophical speculation. Some people reject the Bible because it does not conform to their academic theories. Others reject the Bible because they resist or oppose the Bible's strict moral standards.

Fair judgment requires a person to consider the contents of the Bible with an honest, open, and informed mind that is willing to weigh and accept the resulting truth.

The second necessary basis: *Judge the Bible with facts.*

Fair judgment, and even just plain common sense, requires us to judge the Bible by the same set of facts by which any other book can receive fair and impartial evaluation. We must temporarily turn aside from traditional claims about the Bible made by friend or foe. We must be honest and depend upon irrefutable facts.

If the Bible is the Word of God, common sense declares that its divine source in God and unique content will exalt virtue, truth, and redemption. What the Bible says will prove or disprove its divine origin and validity better than any believer's claim or any unbeliever's rejection.

If the Bible is not the Word of God, common sense declares that its content will vindicate the unbeliever's accusation with substantiated mistakes, errors, and falsehoods.

To repeat for emphasis: This book claims that if the Bible is God's inerrant Word, its true spiritual and factual content will prove its validity. In the same way, if the Bible is not God's inerrant Word, its mistakes, errors, and falsehoods will confirm the unbeliever's accusation.

If the Bible's author is God, alone and separate from all human instrumentality, its unique contents will reveal the divine Source as untarnished by angel or human creature. If the Bible's author is God, using human instruments, the content will reveal both the human personality and the controlling inspiration of deity. If the Bible's author is human, alone or in concert with other humans but separate from deity, common sense declares that the content will rise no higher and sink no lower than the talents and abilities of human sources.

Fair judgment demands that the Bible undergo the same factual judgment given to any other book. Let facts, rather than spiritual devotion or theological bias, determine the decision about the validity of the Bible. Let the Bible's contents, rather than philosophic speculations or unsupported accusations or affirmations, decide its validity. Academic speculations and popular accusations built on intellectual fantasy rather than fact afford no fair standard for any judgment. Ignorance which fortifies its conclusions with the vigor of repeated denials or by immorality, attempting to justify evil actions by rejection of godly standards, likewise provides no basis for judgment.

Permit the Bible to face the court of intellectual honesty and to receive judgment on the basis of universally accepted and irrefutable factors: size, sources, accuracy, prophecy, quality of message, cultural effects, scholarly evaluation, and personal benefits. These are subjects we shall consider in succeeding chapters.

Every book, including the Bible, is a tangible object. The facts about the nature of any object must be explained in order to make a fair judgment. The facts about the contents of any book must definitely be explained in order to make a fair judgment. A fair-minded judgment of the Bible, therefore, must give a reasonable explanation about these critical and factual areas. A judgment that cannot provide such a reasonable explanation about universally acceptable criteria for judgment is unfair to any book, and that must include the Bible.

The Bible, like any other book, deserves an honest, fair, and factual judgment based upon an adequate explanation of the facts about its contents.

On this fair and factual basis we claim the Bible needs no other defender. On the basis of fact, the Bible will prove its own validity. I am certainly not the first person to see this simple fact: *The Bible proves itself.* The renowned Presbyterian theologian Dr. Charles Hodge, a Princeton legend as a scholarly and renowned professor, stated with confidence, "The best evidence of the Bible's being the word of God is to be found between its covers. It proves itself."

The remainder of this book seeks to apply these reasonable tests of factual truth to the contents of the Bible.

CHAPTER FOUR

Test One:
The Size of the Bible

The size of the Bible would appear to afford the least significant factual test as a basis for judgment of its validity. Such was my first assessment. What possible importance could be assigned to so prosaic a factor as size? What significance could size make in the validity of the Bible?

Comparing the size of the Bible to other sacred writings reveals both likeness and difference. They are alike in that each sacred book commands the loyalty of those belonging to that particular faith. They are obviously different in content. They also vary somewhat in size. The Book of Mormon is about half the size of the Bible. The Koran is only a quarter the size of the New Testament. The book of Buddha, which is popular in Japan, is also smaller than the New Testament; the sacred writings of India are much larger than the Bible.

Actually the Bible is quite small in size. Some popular novels and many college texts are larger. Senior citizens carry even large-print editions of the Bible with ease. Little children bring their smaller Bibles to Sunday School. Some pastors use pocket editions in their visitation. Truly, in size the Bible is just a "hand" book.

The Bible is actually a collection of small books of great variety in every aspect: poems, letters, history, typology, prophecies, descriptions, parables, sermons, and proverbs. These small books are grouped together into two main divisions, the Old and New Testaments. Jews accept the Old Testament, which contains thirty-nine books; Christians accept also the New Testament, which contains an additional twenty-seven books. Combined into a single volume, the entire Bible of sixty-six small books is still just a "hand" book in size. It is an appropriate size.

Though first thought concludes that size is unimportant, more careful consideration raises several questions about the Bible that deserve a reasonable answer.

Why is this book the only book that has been printed more than any other sacred or secular writing?

Why has this book been translated into more languages than any other writing in the history of printing? At the beginning of the twenty-first century, the entire Bible had been translated into 371 different languages, the complete New Testament into 960 different languages, and portions of the Bible into yet another 902 languages and dialects—2233 in all. As a result, 90 percent of the people of the world have some part of the Bible in their mother tongue. And the translations continue to increase. Why?

Why has this particular small book survived every effort for its destruction in successive generations? The survival of the Bible impressed Martin Luther so strongly that he wrote, "Mighty potentates have raged against this Book, and sought to destroy and uproot it—Alexander the Great, the princes of Egypt and Babylon, the monarchs of Persia, of Greece, and of Rome, the Emperors Julius and Augustus—but they prevailed nothing. They are gone, while the Book remains, and will remain for ever and ever, perfect and entire, as it was declared at first. Who has thus helped it—who has thus protected it against such mighty forces? No one, surely, but God himself, who is the Master of all things. And 'tis no small miracle how God has so long preserved and protected this Book; for the Devil and the world are sore foes to it." What would justify Luther's amazing statement about this small book?

Who has failed to hear how the very house in which Voltaire predicted the death of the Bible later became the property of the French Bible Society? Why is the Bible now the most wanted book in the very countries formerly dominated by atheistic governments? Despite every attempt to destroy the Bible, this small book survives and thrives.

Why should this book be the subject of more study and discussion than any other writing in history? Dr. James Orr, General Editor of the classic *International Standard Bible Encyclopedia*, emphasized the scholarly interest in this little book, saying, "No book has ever been so minutely studied, has had so many books written on it, has founded so vast a literature of hymns, liturgies, devotional writings, sermons, has been so keenly assailed, has evoked such splendid defenses, as the Bible." What can be the reason for this vast and continuing interest in this book?

Why should this book receive credit for ability to improve the morality of a society? Why would the scholarly John Locke declare, "In morality there are books enough written both by ancient and modern philosophers, but the morality of the Gospel doth so exceed them all that to give a man a full knowledge of true morality I shall send him to no other book than the New Testament." Why would this renowned thinker give this unique credit to this book?

Why does this book receive strong opposition from humanists and the oppression of godless communistic governments?

Although size does not distinquish this handbook, it must possess some unique position and power that distinguishes it from other books. What distinguishes this book from other books?

Undeniably, any book that exerts such international and timeless influence deserves a reasonable explanation and factual evaluation. The Bible has so profoundly influenced man that it is unthinkable to permit an honest person to evade, ignore, or judge lightly the pertinent facts.

In fact, these facts about this "handbook" reinforce the question, "Why should an open-minded person hesitate to make a fair and factual investigation before he passes judgment on the validity of this small 'handbook,' the Bible?"

Don't these amazing facts about this "handbook" become compelling reasons for continued study concerning the validity of the Bible?

CHAPTER FIVE

Test Two:
Diverse Sources Create Bible Unity

Source rates as a significant factor in validating any book's claim for divine origin. The sacred book of Islam, the Koran, or Qur'an (Arabic for "recital") affords an excellent example. Moslems contend that the Koran is the actual words of God revealed to Mohammed between A.D 610 and 632 . Moslems assert that the revelation began when Mohammed was in a cave on Mount Hira and continued until his death. According to Moslem belief, these Arabic oracles are God's very words.

The sacred book of the Mormon church affords another excellent example of a claim for direct revelation. Joseph Smith began having visions at the age of ten. He published the result of these visions in *The Book of Mormon* in 1830. Smith asserted that the book was his correct translation of hieroglyphic writing on golden plates temporarily let down from heaven.

Though different in method and message, both books claim virtually immediate divine origin through revelations made to one person, with God as the single source. In neither of the two examples did the human instrument (supposedly) affect the material in the book. In neither of the two examples does the material in the book reveal the personality of the human instrument.

Contrary to this, the Bible claims to come from an immediate divine source (unaffected, that is, by human personality) *only* in the writing of the Ten Commandments and the writing on the wall at Belshazzar's banquet. The other portions of the Bible admit many varied relationships between the divine source and the human authors.

Indeed, the human sources for the Bible books demonstrate

incredible diversity in the time of writing, in the human instrument's position, personality and relationship with God, and in the literary type of presentation. Instead of the sixty-six books originating from the pen of a single author, the Bible required at least fifty different human writers. What a diverse assembly! Bible authors include kings but also farmers and peasants, physicians but also military leaders, statesmen, tax collectors, sheep herders and prophets, exiles and repatriates.

These human sources claimed equally varied relations to God as the source of what they wrote. Some of the human authors declared that portions of what they wrote were a direct word from God. Isaiah wrote, "Moreover, the word of the Lord came to me." Jeremiah also frequently states, "The word of the Lord came to me." Amos declared, "This is what the Lord says." Micah begins, "The word of the Lord that came to Micah. . . ." The books of Esther and Ruth, however, make no divinity claim. Other Bible books simply chronicle history and make statements about events. None of the authors determined, "The Bible needs another book of the kind that I can write, so I will produce it." There is no indication that the human authors knew that what they were writing would become a part of the Bible. In fact, Simon Peter declared that some of the Old Testament writers did not completely understand the full meaning of their own writings (1 Peter 1:11–12). The Bible's varied human writers were not authors seeking a publisher. As Simon Peter declared, *For prophecy never had its origin in the will of man, but men spoke from God as they were carried along by the Holy Spirit* (2 Peter 1:21). The only common factor that Bible students have found among the fifty or more human writers of the Bible is this inward spiritual guidance by the Spirit of God.

The human writers of the Bible lived and wrote over equally surprising and diverse time periods. Though the book of Job and the works of Moses defy exact time assignment, evidence points to some fifteen hundred or more years before Christ. Some Bible books indicate more exact dates based upon the historical references included by the writer. For example, each section of the prophetic oracles of Ezekiel begins by specifying the year, month, and day.

Several of the prophets followed the example set by Isaiah and dated their writings by the reign of certain kings. No doubt the writings of the Old Testament required a time span of more than one thousand years. Such a vast span of time and position prohibited collaboration for consistency of material among the writers.

Such an extended time span involved an amazing kaleidoscope of human cultures that range from pre-deluge civilization through the early cultures of Egypt and Babylon to the time of Roman world domination. The various books of the Old Testament picture the beginnings of human culture, government, racial divisions, the development of agriculture, industry, and military aggression. Individuals, tribes, and nations march through the centuries on the Biblical pages. Some of the Biblical record describes people who lived in tents and caves, others in palaces and temple sanctuaries. What a panorama of the centuries! What a kaleidoscope of history! What a procession of cultures!

The astounding Bible diversity of human authors, time periods, and cultural patterns increases with the varied types of literature utilized by the human authors. History, poetry, types and symbols, sermons, songs, conversations, proverbs, and visions qualify the Bible for a study of literary forms. Though the Old Testament writers used Hebrew as the basic language of the people, some Aramaic and some Persian words appear in Daniel's writings and elsewhere. It appears that God set no limit in the diversity of authors, types of literature, and historical cultures in the books of the Bible.

What defies the Bible critic is the puzzling fact that unlike any other varied collection of sacred writings, the Bible possesses undeniable unity in theme and teaching. In spite of amazing diversity in time, writer, literary type, and historic culture, scholars agree that the books of the Bible reveal a striking unity of message. Other religions have "bibles" which are collections of heterogeneous materials. Unlike the Bible, these other sacred books may have little or no order, progression, or unifying plan. The Bible stands in sharp contrast. Dr. James Orr, the general editor of *The International Standard Bible Encyclopedia*, emphasizes the importance of this contrast, saying, "It is this aspect of the Bible which constitutes its grand distinction from all collections of sacred writings—the so-called 'bibles' of heathen religions—in the world. These, as the slightest inspection of them shows, have no unity. They are collections of heterogeneous materials, presenting in their collocation no order, progress, or plan. The reason is, that they embody no historical revelation working out a purpose in consecutive stages from germinal beginnings to perfect close. The Bible, by contrast, is a single book because it embodies such a revelation, and exhibits such a purpose. The unity of the book, made up of so many parts, is the attestation of the revelation it contains."

In spite of the long time span of composition and diversity of writers and types of literature, the many separate books of the Bible enable the student to trace an orderly unity in the revelation of God's holy nature and in the progression of divine providence. For example, in the classic book *From Eternity to Eternity*, Eric Sauer uses the historical unity of the Bible to trace the progressive revelation of five teachings: the history of Israel, the history of the temple, the history of Christ, the history of the salvation of the nations, and the history of demonism. No other set of sixty-six books exists in all of human literature that compares with the amazing unity in diversity of the Bible.

Bruce M. Metzer, professor at Princeton Theological Seminary for more than forty years, explains, "The most remarkable feature of the Bible is its unity. The books were written over a period of at least 1200 years by a large number of diverse authors in several languages (Hebrew and Aramaic for the Old Testament and Greek for the New Testament). Yet they all witness fundamentally to the same understanding of the nature of God as (1) a God who acts, (2) a God who redeems, and (3) a God who gives hope."

Other than by recognition that the Bible is God's Word, how can one explain this unique unity?

No other book series—secular or religious—preserves comparable traceable theme unity in spite of extreme diversity in time, culture, and writer. The scholarly J. P. Lange declared, "Viewing the Holy Scriptures as to its effects, its unity proves it to be the Word of God." These scholars, whose reputations span time and culture, agree that the Bible is unique among all sacred books in its amazing unity in diversity because it *is* what it *claims* to be, the Word of God!

G. Campbell Morgan, scholar and preacher, wrote, "We have sixty-six books, as we find them in our Bible, bound together, written over a period of 1500 years, mostly in Hebrew and Greek and some small portions in Aramaic. But it is a library, and that must be insisted upon again and again when studying the Bible."

Fair judgment requires a credible explanation for the Bible's incredible unity in diversity! Only one explanation is credible: the Bible is God's Word.

Is it reasonable to attempt to explain that this diversity of writers achieved this unique unity of message by accident?

Is it reasonable to attempt to explain that this diversity of writers achieved this unique unity of message by crafting what they wrote to fit into the pattern of the centuries?

Is it reasonable to attempt to explain that this diversity of writers achieved this unique unity of purpose through careful choice by an unknown and unnamed council?

Historically, the greatest scholars and the most devout Bible students have accepted only the explanation that this diversity of writers achieved this unique unity of purpose and content because of God's inspiration. They have concluded that this amazing unity vindicates the claim and has demonstrated the fact of the validity of the Bible.

But there is more!

CHAPTER SIX

Test Three:
The Confirmed Historical Accuracy of the Bible

Any book that claims to chronicle a credible record of historical events must undergo the test of accuracy concerning subject matter, times, customs, places, and persons. Because the Bible presents religious truth affords no acceptable reason why it should be allowed to avoid this critical test. The Bible welcomes the test of accuracy regardless of the fact that there were more than 50 authors living over a period of 1500 years in vastly different cultures. If what the diverse human Bible writers record about history fails to accord with authentic facts, then what the Bible teaches about religion becomes questionable. But, if what these Bible authors recorded about history accords with authenticated facts, then doesn't what the Bible teaches about religion deserve acceptance as valid?

The Bible record has faced and continues to face multiple tests of its historical accuracy made by skeptics and archaeologists. Nevertheless, the Bible has earned a unique record of historical accuracy unrivaled among religious books.

Let us first consider some earlier archaeological examples of Biblical testing and resulting scholarly conclusions. For example, consider how in the nineteenth century skeptics and archaeologists accused the Bible of fictitious statements when it made mention of the Hittites because no non-Biblical evidence existed for such a nation. But after 1906 the digs made at Hattushash—which proved to be the capital city of the Hittite nation—changed the alleged Biblical myth into accurate historical fact. Archaeology revealed that the Hittites had existed as a powerful nation. Excavations completely authenticated the Biblical record. Indeed, one Egyptian tablet actually recorded a fierce battle between Ramses II and the

Hittites at Kadesh on the Orontes River. The Bible record was verified as accurate history.

Early scholars had condemned the historical accuracy of Bible statements concerning Belshazzar because no non-Biblical records listed this ruler. But in 1853 archaeologists found an inscription in Ur that confirmed the Bible record, showing that Belshazzar reigned with his father, Nabonides. Archeology has continued to confirm Biblical records. The scholarly Dr. J. O. Kinnaman affirmed this amazing Biblical historical accuracy, saying, "Of the hundreds of thousands of artifacts found by the archaeologists, not one has ever been discovered that contradicts or denies one word, phrase, clause, or sentence of the Bible, but always confirms and verifies the fact of the Bible record."

Dr. Nelson Glueck, considered the outstanding Jewish archeologist of the twentieth century, added his confirmation of Bible accuracy in his book *Rivers in the Desert*, saying, "It may be stated categorically that no archeological discovery has ever controverted a Biblical reference. Scores of archeological findings have been made which confirm in clear outline or in exact detail historical statements in the Bible."

The more that the honest inquirer considers the stretch of history covered by the Biblical record and the diversity of authors who wrote the Bible, the more amazing is this record of Biblical historical accuracy.

Dr. Werner Keller, author of *The Bible in History* and of the pictorial volume *The Bible as History in Pictures*, made this challenging evaluation of the historical accuracy of the Bible: "As a journalist I have been for many years exclusively concerned with the results of modern science and research. . . . These sensational reports—and, indeed, in view of the significance of these finds it is not too much to use the word 'sensational'—awakened in me the desire to come to closer grips with Biblical archaeology, the most recent and, generally speaking, least known province in the field of investigation into the ancient world. I therefore ransacked German and foreign literature for a comprehensive and intelligible summary of the results of previous research. I found none, for there was none to find. So I went to the sources myself in the libraries of many lands—aided in this bit of real detective work by my wife's enthusiasm—and collected all the hitherto scientifically established results of investigation which were to be found in the learned works of Biblical archaeologists."

The result of Dr. Keller's research was published by William Morrow and Company of New York in 1956 under the title *The Bible in History*. The authoritative volume was the fifteenth printing, a fully revised edition published in 1964. Dr. Keller concludes his introduction with this affirmation concerning archaeology's contribution to the validity of the Bible record: "In view of the overwhelming and well-tested evidence now available, as I thought of the skeptical criticism which from the eighteenth century onward would fain have demolished the Bible altogether, there kept hammering in my brain this one sentence: 'The Bible was right, after all!'"

In 1929 I heard Dr. Robert Dick Wilson, the renowned Professor of Semitic philology at Princeton Theological Seminary, tell his students, "I have acquired knowledge of every language spoken by the nations listed in Genesis. Not one Bible statement has ever been proven false." Dr. Wilson's written affirmation challenges the skeptic: "After forty-five years of scholarly research in Biblical textual studies and in language study, I have come now to the conviction that no man knows enough to assail the truthfulness of the Old Testament. When there is sufficient documentary evidence to make an investigation, the statements of the Bible, in the original text, have stood the test." This scholarly affirmation summarizes the proven fact of the unique accuracy of the Biblical record. No other sacred book equals the Bible for historical accuracy.

The science of archaeology has continued to verify the historical accuracy of the Bible by factual and external evidence gained by scientific excavations. Archeology has continued to confirm that the Bible is unique in its accurate historical statements. No matter what the accuracy test, the Bible has vindicated its validity without failure.

Harry Thomas Frank has written an excellent summation of the historical accuracy of the Bible in *Discovering the Biblical World*, saying, "If, for example, the recovery of ancient Middle Eastern life had shown that the Biblical writers were either incorrect in what history they do report or had sought to falsify it, there would be serious repercussions concerning the veracity of other Biblical statements. Just the opposite has in fact happened. Archaeological recovery of ancient life has tended at point after point to show with what faithfulness the Biblical writers recorded contemporary events. This indicates that the Bible as a primary historical document is a trustworthy guide to those events and situations which it describes."

Though these affirmations are from scholars who passed away decades ago, archaeological digs have since become more and more numerous and precise. In fact, both archaeological and Biblical scholarship have made marked progress in the past century and continue to do so. Let us consider some contemporary facts relative to the historical accuracy of the Bible.

One needs to be aware that, today, Biblical confirmation no longer dominates archaeological investigation. Both universities and archaeological societies specialize in digs that relate to varied ancient civilizations. Motivation focuses upon a broader objective than Biblical information. An example of this is the statement of Israel's leading Biblical minimalist, Israel Finkelstein, who declared that the Bible is irrelevant as direct historical testimony concerning the rise of Israel. In making this statement, Dr. Finkelstein indicates that his motivation is apart from either proving or disproving the Biblical record. He is simply seeking what the archaeological record will reveal in addition to the plenitude of present findings that have already established Biblical accuracy. In short, secular science has little or no interest in Biblical confirmation.

Consider for a moment a fraction of the examples of this plenitude of Biblical confirmation by archaeology. First, there is the record of *events*:

* The walls of the Temple of Amun confirm Pharaoh Shishak's attack on Israel recorded in 1 Kings 14:25–26.
* The Mesha Inscription confirms Moab's revolt against Israel recorded in 2 Kings 3:4–27.

❖ The palace walls of Sargon II confirm the defeat of Ashdod as recorded in Isaiah 20:1.
❖ The Babylon Ration records confirm the captivity of Jehoiachin as recorded in 2 Kings 24:15–16; 25:27–30.
❖ Freedom for Jewish captives by Cyrus the Great (substantiating Ezra 1:1–4) is confirmed by the Cyrus Cylinder.

Consider also how archaeology has confirmed *places* where the Bible records various events:

❖ the Temple of Baal in Shechem
❖ the pools of Gibeon and of Heshbon and of Samaria
❖ the water tunnel beneath Jerusalem dug by King Hezekiah
❖ King Belshazzar's royal palace in Babylon
❖ the royal palace of Susa (with memory of Esther and Mordecai)
❖ the foundation of the synagogue in Capernaum

Consider a few of the *persons* that archaeology has confirmed so that the Bible and archaeological findings walk in harmony:

❖ Jehu
❖ Hazael
❖ Sargon II
❖ Esarhaddon
❖ Merodach-Baladan
❖ Darius I
❖ Herod Agrippa I
❖ Pilate
❖ Caiaphas

Hugh Williamson, the Regius Professor at Oxford University, declared that to deny the "historical bedrock" of the Bible is perverse. Shmuel Ahituv, of Ben-Gurion University of the Negev, contends, "Let us admit that the fog covering the origins and the early phases in the history of ancient Israel has not yet dispersed. The Bible is still our most important source of information for this study." Without diminishing the motivation of the minimalist archaeologists to seek non-Biblical data, these scholars are emphasizing the incredible amount of information that has already established the historical accuracy of the Biblical record. Jonathan Tubb of the British Museum declared that it was "unnecessarily obtuse to look further afield for [the] catalyst [that transformed the self-perception of Canaanites to Israelites] than the literary traditions of the Exodus and conquest preserved in the Old Testament."

An additional argument for the accuracy of the Bible is what it does *not* contain. Here is one clear example.

Is the Exodus story simply "folklore," as various modern contrarians suggest? Alan Millard, Rankin Reader in Hebrew and Ancient Semitic Languages at the University of Liverpool, England, while not specifically arguing for the composition of the book of Exodus as early as conservative scholars do, nevertheless (in the July/August 2000 issue of *Biblical Archaeology Review*), in a sidebar, says: "I am speaking here simply of the extant manuscript evidence. As I point out in my article, the lack of Aramaic, Persian or Greek vocabulary and grammar in Exodus suggests that the text is earlier than the Babylonian Exile (sixth century B.C.). As I further point out, historical details in Exodus indicate that it accurately preserves information from the times it describes: the Late Bronze Age, or about a thousand years earlier than the oldest surviving manuscripts of Exodus (mid–third century B.C.)."

I am admittedly not an archaeological scholar, but I am unwilling to challenge the consensus of a long history of investigation by Biblical and archaeological scholarship. With almost no exceptions in a rich heritage, scholars have affirmed the evidence in archaeology and philology that the Biblical record is historically accurate. In contemporary science the findings give ample evidences of the accuracy of the Biblical record. Even in the debate with the minimalist, the issue seems to center upon what is the incentive for additional excavations rather than the factual accuracy of what has already been uncovered.

Archaeological discoveries have continued to confound skeptics who, with little knowledge of secular history or of the Bible record, glibly assert that the Bible is full of mistakes. The most knowledgeable scholars testify to the mass of evidence that demonstrates the historical accuracy of the Bible record. And when one remembers that the Bible was written by more than two score of authors, many of them completely untrained in history, the skeptic's cavil is irresponsible.

Fair judgment requires a reasonable explanation for the unique accuracy of the Bible's record of human history. How can any explanation that denies that the Bible is God's Word account for the historical accuracy of the Bible? No one has even dared to suggest the fanciful theory that some unknown scholar or group of scholars edited the Biblical record and removed all the mistakes. History records no such editorial staff. Nor has any school of thought dared to present the ridiculous theory that this diverse group of human Bible writers, who wrote over such a long time span, possessed a human ability—an ability shared by no other humans— that enabled them to make no mistakes. The Bible writers were not superhuman.

Fair judgment or just ordinary common sense can accept the explanation that the inspiration of God protected the human Bible writers from mistakes because the Bible is what it claims to be: the Word of God.

What other alternative is available? This unique historical accuracy gives the Bible a unique validity.

Knowledge of such scholarly confirmations concerning the historical accuracy of the Bible enabled Dr. W. A. Criswell in 1969 to affirm publicly, boldly, and with no fear of contradiction, "There has been no shred of archaeological evidence yet discovered that contradicts the Word of God."

And there are still no contradictions! In fact, in a feature *U.S. News & World Report* (October 25, 1999) article titled "Is the Bible True?" Jeffery L. Sheler, author of *Is the Bible True?*, states, "Before the discovery of the 'House of David' inscription at Dan in 1993, it had become fashionable in some academic circles to dismiss the David stories as an invention of priestly propagandists who were trying to dignify Israel's past after the Babylonian exile. But as Tel Aviv University minimalist archeologist Israel Finkelstein admits, 'Biblical nihilism collapsed overnight with the discovery of the David inscription.'"

Every honest reader should be willing to ask himself this critical question: When so many recognized scholars and archeologists have testified to the historical accuracy of the Bible record for more than two centuries, how can I be egotistical enough to claim that these authorities are incorrect and that I have discovered that the Bible is full of mistakes and errors?

But there is more!

CHAPTER SEVEN

Test Four:
The Bible's Confirmed Fulfilled Prophecies

The dictionary gives the word "prophecy" three major meanings: one, the vocation of a prophet; two, an inspired utterance of a prophet; three, a declaration of something to come. Our present purpose limits discussion to the predictive ministry of foretelling the future. Fair judgment of Biblical prophetic prediction requires a firm standard for testing true prophecy, an appreciation of the diversity in the life and work of Bible prophets, a recognition of the amount of Biblical prophecy, and examples of detailed prophecy with specific fulfillment.

1. A Sure Standard for Testing True Prophecy

The Bible established a strict and uncompromising standard for testing the validity of any prophecy: the future fulfillment must equate with the prophetic prediction.

The Bible asks a negative question: *How can we know when a message has not been spoken by the Lord?* The Bible answer gives the most rigid test: *If what a prophet proclaims in the name of the Lord does not take place or come true, that is a message the Lord has not spoken. That prophet has spoken presumptuously. Do not be afraid of him* (Deuteronomy 18:21–22).

Prophecy could face no more firm nor demanding test than that which the Bible raises. The Bible test allowed no compromise. The fulfillment must correspond to the prediction in time, place, person, and even detailed circumstances. No evaluation can boast a higher standard or a more sure test. Yet the Bible placed every Biblical prophet and his prediction under this uncompromising requirement for validation.

2. *The Amazing Diversity of the Bible Prophets*

Though the Old Testament speaks of a "school of the prophets," God used a variety of people apart from any special training to serve as Bible prophets. Prophets whose writings are preserved as a part of the Old Testament present a profile of complete cultural and educational diversity. None claimed to be psychic or trained in prophecy. Careful study establishes the fact that the one bond of human likeness in the prophets was that they were God-called. Consider the godly Samuel, the princely Isaiah, the rural Amos, the statesman Daniel, the weeping Jeremiah, the sorrowing Hosea. Each prophet differed widely from all the others. None had special training for the position. Each had simply responded to God's call.

As the prophets differ, so do their predictions; yet no prophecy is contradictory to others. All progressively unfold God's plan and program for human history through a God-called and God-inspired spokesman. Prophecy provides another unique example of unity despite diversity.

3. *The Unique Amount of Bible Prophecy*

The amount of Bible prophecy has captivated the attention of students. Dr. J. Barton Payne has recorded and published the results of an exhaustive study of Bible predictions. He reached the conclusion that out of 31,124 Bible verses, 8,352 are predictive. No other book, sacred or secular, approaches the Bible record for the sheer amount of prophecy.

Twenty-eight-and-one-half percent of the Old Testament and twenty-one-and-one-half percent of the New Testament are predictive. Counting repeats in different Bible books, Dr. Payne found 1,817 predictions. On this basis, the Bible tests its own validity nearly two thousand times by the strict Biblical standard for judging the validity of a prophecy. No other book, sacred or secular, has substantiated belief in the accuracy of its predictions by this rigid Biblical test of validity.

4. *Examples of Bible Prophecy and Fulfillment*

Begin by considering prophecies made in the Bible whose fulfillment has been recorded in non-Biblical history. Ezekiel 26:3–

5, 7 declares Tyre's destruction as follows: *". . . therefore this is what the Sovereign Lord says: I am against you, O Tyre, and I will bring many nations against you, like the sea casting up its waves. They will destroy the walls of Tyre and pull down her towers; I will scrape away her rubble and make her a bare rock. Out in the sea she will become a place to spread fishnets. . . . I am going to bring against Tyre Nebuchadnezzar king of Babylon. . . ."*

In the sixth century Nebuchadnezzar partially destroyed the old city of Tyre, the mainland part. Then in 332 B.C. Alexander the Great scraped its ruins into the Mediterranean to make a causeway so that his army could destroy the remaining island city, thereby completing the prophecy's fulfillment in every detail.

When Jeremiah saw his nation led into captivity, God inspired him to promise that the captivity would end in seventy years. Jeremiah prophesied, saying, *This is what the Lord says: "When seventy years are completed for Babylon, I will come to you and fulfill my gracious promise to bring you back to this place. For I know the plans I have for you,"* declares the Lord (Jeremiah 29:10–11). What prophesy promised, history has recorded to the exact date.

When Jesus' disciples pointed out the massive stones of Jerusalem, the Lord prophesied, saying, *"Do you see all these things? I tell you the truth, not one stone here will be left on another; every one will be thrown down"* (Matthew 24:2). In 70 A.D. the Roman general Titus and his army completely fulfilled Jesus' prophecy.

In each example the Biblical prophecy was fulfilled in history.

These three examples of prophecy and fulfillment, selected from the imposing array designated by Dr. Payne, demonstrate that exact fulfillment distinguishes the Bible prophecies from all other prophetic writings. What the Bible prophet predicted equated accurately with the fulfillment.

No other writing—secular or religious—compares with the Biblical books in the number of the fulfillments of predictions of the future. Past history has already vindicated hundreds of Bible predictions, and even more importantly, has contradicted none. The Bible is unique in all literature in the area of prophecy made and precisely fulfilled.

The Chain-Reference Bible utilizes the results of thirty-one years of Bible study by Dr. Frank Charles Thompson. Included in this monumental system is a list of thirty-eight Old Testament prophecies and their New Testament fulfillment in the earthly ministry of Jesus. Hundreds of years separated the enunciation of the prophecy and its fulfillment. For example, consider only seven specific prophecies:

1. The place of Jesus' birth, Micah 5:2.
2. The time of Jesus' Birth, Daniel 9:25.
3. Rejection by the Jews, Isaiah 53:3.
4. Crucified with sinners, Isaiah 53:12.
5. Hands and feet pierced, Psalm 22:16.
6. Bones not broken, Psalm 34:20.
7. Resurrected, Psalm 16:10.

Not only these examples but all the other prophesies were fulfilled so accurately that Jesus could instruct his disciples, saying, *"This is what I told you while I was still with you: Everything must be fulfilled that is written about me in the Law of Moses, the Prophets and the Psalms"* (Luke 24:44).

Because Jesus fulfilled completely the Old Testament prophecies concerning the Messiah's birth, life-ministry, death and resurrection, Peter, Paul and Apollos were able to use them to prove to their hearers that Jesus was indeed the Messiah. In all of human history the life of no person other than Jesus has matched what the prophets stated. In fact, a modern statistician declared that the possibility of any one life matching all the prophecies is astronomical. Only Jesus has made this fulfillment. The records of Jesus' life chronicled the exact fulfillment of what the Bible prophets had predicted. Two thousand years after Jesus fulfilled these prophecies, present-day Christians are able to use the same prophecies and their fulfillment by Jesus to prove that he is the Messiah. No other person has duplicated or could duplicate Jesus' record of prophetic fulfillment.

Skeptics have attempted in vain to discredit the accuracy of Biblical predictions. Every accusation has resulted in another vindication by the strict standard that the Bible has established. In two thousand years no book, secular or sacred, has rivaled the Bible for amount and fulfillment of prophecy.

Fair judgment asks the question, "How can the unique accuracy of the Bible predictions be explained without accepting the claim that the Bible is the Word of God?" Accidental coincidence could not possibly account for the mass of Biblical prediction and subsequent fulfillment. The accuracy of Biblical prophecy defies any reasonable explanation other than that the Bible is what it claims to be: the Word of God.

The accuracy of Biblical prophecy accepts no alternative explanation because Biblical prophecy actually requires and demonstrates the validity of the Bible.

The facts about the unique prophecies of the Bible enabled Dr. W. A. Criswell to make another bold affirmation, saying, "No man with a fair and open mind could read the prophecies in the Old Testament and follow the types and symbols of the worship of the Hebrews without seeing that it all was inspired by the Lord of heaven and recorded according to the dictation of the Spirit."

No critical scholar, humanistic philosopher, or materialistic scientist has produced an acceptable and logical alternative!

And there is more!

CHAPTER EIGHT

Test Five:
The Quality of the Message: Old Testament Holiness

All books, but more especially all sacred writings, must undergo the test of the ethical quality of their messages. The minimum test must include an answer to the following question: Is the message a unique, original, and worthy revelation or is the message an imitation or a copy of some other writing of inferior quality?

Human authors, including those of the Hebrew nation, have produced books about religious subjects and even about Hebrew history that are not included in the canon. These Jewish writings, such as the *Apocrypha*, have failed to pass the minimum canonical test. Others have failed by having authorship claims that have proven false.

The thirty-nine Old Testament books contrast with all other religious writings in one clear aspect—the quality in their message. The unique message of "deity holiness" distinguishes the Old Testament books from all other religious writings. No other writing, secular or sacred, can claim to have originated or communicated the Bible's unique revelation of ethical righteousness. Even the Koran falls short. The Old Testament presents the first and the unique revelation of one holy God who requires holiness in his worshipers and provides a way to obtain it.

The Old Testament Revelation of Holiness Is Unique

The Old Testament receives a deserved recognition for its unique presentation of holiness both in the nature of God and in God's standards for human character and conduct. No competitors for this revelation exist.

1. The Old Testament reveals the one God who is holy.

Though the Old Testament human writers lived in the midst of cultures whose many gods exalted sexual promiscuity, violence, deceit, child abuse and degradation of women, these Biblical writers presented the unique message of one God of holy character who rewarded righteousness and punished iniquity.

This quality of its holy God makes the Old Testament unique among all religious books, whatever the culture. No other Oriental or Western nation projected the concept of a *holy* god. The Mesopotamians among whom Abraham lived reveled in sexual orgies in worshiping their deities. The Canaanite tribes worshiped the god of the lust of the bull. The sun and moon gods of Egypt fell far short of possessing holiness of character or requiring holiness in mankind. Greek philosophy never achieved the ideal of holiness. The gods of Rome magnified the human lusts for sexual immorality and oppressive power. Among all mankind, no other nation or people invented, conceived, or taught that God was holy and righteous— none except the Hebrews. Of all sacred literature, only the Bible teaches the truth of one God who is holy and eternally righteous. This unique message requires an adequate explanation. How did the multiple Old Testament writers, over centuries, originate and proclaim a concept of holiness that is different from all other literature?

2. The Old Testament reveals that God requires holiness in mankind.

The Old Testament revelation raised a unique standard of holiness for human character and conduct. Whereas non-Biblical religions projected human passions into the character and conduct of their gods, the Old Testament writers called for human character and conduct to be patterned after the holiness of God: *"I am the Lord your God; consecrate yourselves, and be holy, because I am holy"* (Lev. 11:44).

The holiness that the Old Testament required in the character and conduct of God's worshipers related to every aspect of human life. Not only religious ceremony but personal, family, business, political, and recreational aspects of daily living required conformity to the holiness of God. This unique religious requirement of holiness produced a quality of ethical life that included the rights of women and children, slaves, and properties. The Old Testament writers revealed and projected a unique system of God-given laws and ordinances that would affect all future generations.

Many world leaders have expressed the ethical benefits of this revelation. Henry Ward Beecher declared that "the Bible stands alone in human literature in its elevated conception of manhood, in character and conduct." Bacon declared that "there never was found, in any age of the world, either religion or law that did so highly exalt the public good as the Bible." Coleridge declared that "for more than a thousand years the Bible, collectively taken, has gone hand in hand with civilization, science, law; in short, with the moral and intellectual cultivation of the species, always supporting and often leading the way." While such quotations could be multiplied, these adequately state that this concept of holiness in God and man is unique to the Bible. It is an established fact that no other secular or sacred book deserves credit as a source of the concept of holiness in God or man—only the Bible.

The actions of the chief characters of the Old Testament contradict any possibility that the concept of holiness was the natural outgrowth of their thought. Moses was a murderer, Abraham and Isaac were lying deceivers, Jacob was a cheat, the patriarch heads of ten of the twelve tribes sold their own brother into slavery, the Hebrews were a rebellious nation, David was an adulterer and a murderer. The Biblical revelations could not have arisen from the Hebrew culture or population. The Biblical revelations were possible only by what the Bible claims. The unique concept of holiness gives evidence that validates the Bible's claim.

The Bible's unique revelation of holiness in God and God's requirement for holiness in humanity evidently originates from a source above, not from a rebellious and evil humanity.

No accident of heredity or environment can explain how this unique concept of holiness developed in no other people, culture or religion, but in the diverse writers of the Bible.

That the forty diverse writers of the Old Testament, over a time span of more than one thousand years, could collaborate in developing the concept of Biblical holiness is an evident impossibility.

No acceptable alternative has been found to the explanation that God revealed himself and his righteous requirements to the human writers of the Old Testament and, therefore, that the Bible is what it claims to be: the Word of God.

And there is more!

CHAPTER NINE

Test Six:
The Jesus Test: Fourfold Reality

The unique evidences of the Old Testament (theme unity, historical accuracy, prophetic fulfillment, character holiness) come to a mind-boggling climax in the New Testament revelation about Jesus. Recorded in Luke 24:44 is Jesus' claim that he is the theme of the Old Testament, that he gives testimony to its historical reality, that he is the proof of its prophetic fulfillment, and that he is the personification of its holiness. Jesus teaches: *"This is what I told you while I was still with you. Everything must be fulfilled that is written about me in the Law of Moses, the Prophets and the Psalms."* Jesus is teaching that the Old Testament vindicates the reality of his claims and that he, as the personification of Old Testament teaching, vindicates the Old Testament. In short, Jesus and the Old Testament stand or fall together.

Many world religions include some person who originates, personifies, or to some degree represents the quality of its message. For example, the names of Buddha, Confucius, Mohammed, Joseph Smith, Mary Baker Eddy, will identify a specific religion or cult. While none of these religions ventures to risk judgment of their message on the basis of the total quality of character and conduct of the associated personality, none can escape some degree of judgment on the personification test.

Certainly, and to a greater extent than any of those listed, the New Testament rests its claim for validity upon the person, character, work, promises, claims, death, resurrection, and ascension of Jesus Christ. Jesus is the personification test because Jesus originates and personifies the New Testament's full and final revelation of the God of the entire Bible. The unique revelation of holiness in the Old

Testament comes to a fulfilling climax in the New Testament revelation of the Lord Jesus Christ. No other religious writing, no ancient or modern philosophy, no secular or sacred literature has ever conceived or presented anything that compares with the New Testament revelation of the Word become flesh. Jesus told Philip, "... *anyone who has seen me has seen the Father*" (John 14:9). The Apostle Paul wrote to the church at Colosse that Jesus *is the image of the invisible God*. What the Old Testament could express about the holiness of God only in words, the New Testament portrays in the person of Jesus: *In the past God spoke to our forefathers through the prophets at many times and in various ways, but in these last days he has spoken to us by his Son. . . . The Son is the radiance of God's glory and the exact representation of his being* (Hebrews 1:1–3). Therefore, not only the New Testament but the validity of the entire Bible stands or falls on Jesus' true personification of the holy God.

The New Testament reveals Jesus as a human being having the holy character of Almighty God—serving humanity in a ministry of perfect righteousness and redemptive love. What the Old Testament stated about the holiness of God in words, Jesus realizes in physical earthly life. The New Testament declares that Jesus demonstrated in his sinless life, his sacrificial death, and his triumphant resurrection the wondrous revelation that the holy God loves sinful man and offers free redemption to undeserving humanity—received by simply repenting of sin and trusting in Jesus as divine Savior. In all of human history the Bible doctrine of redemption is unique. No other secular or sacred literature has conceived of God's gracious and redemptive holiness as portrayed in the Old Testament. No such literature has conceived of God's gracious and redemptive love and redemptive grace as exemplified in the New Testament by Jesus' life, death, and resurrection. The New Testament portrays Jesus as the God-man, the one and only sufficient Mediator between the holy God and unholy man. The New Testament reveals Jesus as the perfect image of God, the perfect Example of holy manhood, and the perfect Redeemer of lost mankind.

The validity of this presentation of Jesus, therefore, becomes the supreme test for the validity of the Bible. The entire collection of sixty-six books hinges upon the validity of the New Testament Jesus who claims to fulfill the Old Testament types and prophecies and, in the New Testament, to personify the full revelation of Almighty God. If the personification of Jesus stands, the Bible stands; if the personification of Jesus crumbles, the validity of the Bible crumbles.

The Bible's validity, therefore, hangs upon the validity of four facts in the New Testament portrayal of Jesus:

Fact One: The New Testament is the record of the life and influence of a person named Jesus who actually lived on earth as a historical figure.

Fact Two: The New Testament is the record of a person named Jesus who personified in his life, death, resurrection, and ascension the perfection of the Son of God.

Fact Three: The New Testament is the record of a person named Jesus who accepted worship as deity from his contemporaries.

Fact Four: The New Testament is the record of a person named Jesus who claimed to be deity as the Son of God.

The truth of these four facts about Jesus is crucial to the validity of the Bible and Christianity. The Bible and the Christian faith stand firm or crumble upon the foundation of the validity of the New Testament record about Jesus as the Son of God.

Other religions and cults may refuse, reject, or fail the personification test. Not so with the Bible. The written Word and the Living Word must agree. The validity of the Bible depends on the validity of Jesus' historical and actual personification of God in character, conduct, and redemptive death, burial, resurrection, and ascension.

Let us now investigate these four critical and decisive tests of the New Testament record.

CHAPTER TEN

The Sixth Test Continued:
Reality #1. Jesus Lived in History

The fact that Jesus actually lived in history now defies any reasonable doubt. In addition to the New Testament record, the most reliable ancient secular sources attest to this historical fact: Jesus lived! Whether Jesus receives acceptance as deity or as human, the fact that such a person lived stands as an indisputable fact.

Multiple varied and tested evidences confirm Jesus' earthly existence. To deny that Jesus lived on earth is to deny the validity of factual historical records. The New Testament is a record of the life and influence of an actual person named Jesus.

The existence of Christianity itself offers proof of the fact that Jesus lived. If Buddhism gives proof to the fact that Buddha lived, and it does, then global Christianity is a proof that Jesus lived. If Confucianism is a proof that Confucius lived, and it is, then global Christianity is a proof that Jesus lived.

Unbelievers may reject the New Testament's claim for divine inspiration but they cannot reasonably reject the New Testament as an accurate historical documentary source. Scholars have recognized that the New Testament record of customs, religious movements, political figures, countries and cities, times and places, establishes its historical validity. Skeptics may show disagreement with Luke or Paul by their refusing to worship Jesus but skeptics cannot deny their scholarship or ability to record factual history. Skeptics may deny the theology of Luke's record, but denial of the historical accuracy of his record of sayings and events requires more than denial. For example, consider the scholarly vindication of the New Testament record by Sir Frederic G. Kenyon, the director of the British Museum: "The interval, then, between the dates of original composition and the earliest extant evidence becomes so small as to be in fact negligible, and the last foundation for any doubt that the Scriptures have come down to us substantially as they were written has now been removed. Both the authenticity and the general integrity of the books of the New Testament may be regarded as finally established." The New Testament record proves that Jesus lived, proves it beyond the possibility of reasonable doubt.

Secular records, recognized by contemporary scholars, also prove that Jesus lived. Though these records fail to vindicate the claims of theology, they afford incontestable proof of the fact that Jesus actually lived on earth.

1. Flavius Josephus, the first century Jewish historian, stated in *Antiquities of the Jews*: "About this time lived Jesus, a man full of wisdom, if indeed one may call Him a man. For He was the doer of incredible things, and the teacher of such as gladly received the truth. He thus attracted to Himself many Jews and many of the Gentiles. He was the Christ. On the accusation of the leading men of our people, Pilate condemned Him to death upon the cross; nevertheless those who had previously loved Him still remained faithful to Him. For on the third day He again appeared to them living, just as, in addition to a thousand other marvelous things, prophets sent by God had foretold. And to the present day the race of those who call themselves Christians after Him has not ceased."

2. Suetonius, the Roman biographer, in *Nero*, wrote during the reign of Nero, saying, "Punishment [by Nero] was inflicted on Christians, a class of men given to a new and mischievous superstition."

3. Tacitus, a distinguished historian of the second century, in *Annals*, having remarked that Nero attempted to blame the burning of Rome on Christians, wrote, "But the pernicious superstition, repressed for a time, broke out again, not only in Judea, where the mischief originated, but through the city of Rome also. . . ."

4. Lucian, a Roman writer who scorned Christians, described Christ in *The Passing of Peregrinus* by calling Christ "the man who was crucified in Palestine because he introduced this new cult into the world."

The fact that Jesus Christ actually lived receives confirmation not only from the New Testament but from recognized secular sources whose authors were actually enemies of Christians. These secular sources, plus the New Testament records, plus the factual history of the Christian movement, face the skeptic with this dilemma: *one*, he must admit that Jesus Christ actually lived, or *two*, he must deny the reliability of universally recognized historical data. To deny the reliability of the fact that Jesus lived would deny the reliability of all historical records. There is far more historical proof for the fact that Jesus lived than for the fact that Pontius Pilate lived to sentence him to the cross. In fact, the historian Philip Schaff declared, "It would take more than a Jesus to invent a Jesus."

The truth that Jesus was a historical person is beyond reasonable contest! The New Testament is a record of the life and influence of a person named Jesus who lived on earth.

CHAPTER ELEVEN

The Sixth Test Continued:
Reality #2. Jesus Personified Unique Perfection

No other character in human history or imaginative literature compares with the Jesus set forth in the New Testament. He differs from them in birth, life, works, death, resurrection, and ascension. While his humanity is visible, his unique perfection is inescapable. Skeptics may deny that Jesus actually possessed the perfection ascribed to him, but the fact that the New Testament person named Jesus demonstrated perfection is the verdict of history.

Examples of Affirmation of Jesus' Perfection

The sincere and virtually universal affirmation of the New Testament portrayal of Jesus as a person of perfection has blazed a unique record of growing glory through the centuries. W. E. Channing expressed what millions have thought of Jesus when he wrote, "No other fame can be compared with that of Jesus. He has a place in the human heart that no one who has ever lived has in any measure rivaled."

The New Testament Jesus stands as the central personality in the Christian faith. Though Roman Catholics may venerate Mary and crown Peter with sainthood, they worship only Jesus. Though Paul deserves honor as the church's greatest Christian missionary statesman, that Apostle crowns Jesus as his Lord and Savior. Persons, doctrines, and institutions in and out of Christendom acknowledge that Jesus stands preeminent in his perfection.

Moreover, the New Testament Jesus, whether historical or fictional, has received this affirmation for two thousand years. Two statements by extremely opposite individuals illuminate the amazing mystery in the facts of Jesus' brief life. Considering the continuing power of Jesus in human history, Napoleon declared, "Alexander, Caesar, Charlemagne and I myself have founded empires; but upon what do these creations of our genius depend? Upon force. Jesus alone founded His empire upon love; and to this very day millions would die for Him."

In striking contrast, the godly Fenelon summarized the humble circumstances and contemporary rejection of Jesus: "Jesus Christ was born in a stable; He was obliged to fly into Egypt; thirty years of His life were spent in a workshop; He suffered hunger, thirst, and weariness; He was poor, despised, and miserable; He taught the doctrines of heaven, and no one would listen. The great and the wise persecuted and took Him, subjected Him to frightful torments, treated Him as a slave, and put Him to death between two malefactors, having preferred to give liberty to a robber rather than to suffer Him to escape. Such was the life which our Lord chose. . . ."

Honesty must admit that both of these amazing evaluations are equally factual about the New Testament portrait. Neither history nor literature provide any comparison to the New Testament record of the perfection of Jesus.

In the New Testament record Jesus' life and love suffered no flaw or fault. Jesus demonstrated a life of perfection.

An unknown author has given a graphic summary of Jesus' place in the mind of mankind: "Christ was placed midmost in the world's history; and in that central position He towers like some vast mountain to heaven—the farther slope stretching backward toward the creation, the hither slope toward the consummation of all things. The ages before look to Him with prophetic gaze; the ages since behold Him by historic faith; by both He is seen in common as the brightness of the Father's glory, and the unspeakable gift of God to the race."

Whether the New Testament writers were justified in describing Jesus as perfect is a matter for personal decision. The fact that the New Testament writers did portray Jesus as perfection is indisputable. And Jesus' perfection is so unique that time has produced no competitor.

Examples of the Effect of Accepting the Perfect Jesus

Only after many years did I remember what I was told about Lew Wallace, the author of *Ben Hur*. According to the story that was told to me, Wallace was associated with a group of agnostics who were interested in disproving the Bible. Because Wallace was a renowned author, he accepted the suggestion that he write a novel that would destroy the Jesus myth. In order to write the novel, Wallace was compelled to study the New Testament portrayal of Jesus. As he studied the Gospels, the New Testament records convinced him of the authenticity of the presentation of Jesus. Wallace accepted Jesus as his Savior and Lord and wrote *Ben Hur*, the greatest novel in affirmation of the New Testament portrait of Jesus that has ever been written.

Dr. Young-Ki Cho, the pastor of the largest church in the history of Christianity, shared with me this personal experience: "At the end of the Korean War, I was a 17-year-old lad with Buddhist faith of a Buddhist family. I was sitting in the street in a weakened and hopeless condition, for I was dying with tuberculosis. Someone came by and handed me a New Testament. I knew nothing about the Christian faith but I started to read the New Testament. As I read, I became convinced that Jesus was who and what the New Testament claimed, able both to heal and to save. During the following forty years I have proved that the New Testament picture of Jesus is true."

Only three responses are logically possible to the claim that the New Testament records the truth concerning the perfection of Jesus:

1. The description is only reverential and fictional.
2. The description is a deliberate deception.
3. The description is a true and unembellished account.

Only one can be true!

When Horace Bushnell faced this choice concerning the unique perfection of Jesus, he made his choice, saying, "When has the world seen a phenomenon like this?—a lonely uninstructed youth, coming from amid the moral darkness of Galilee, even more distinct from His age, and from everything around Him, than a Plato would be rising up in some wild tribe in Oregon, assuming thus a position at the head of the world and maintaining it, for eighteen centuries, by the pure self-evidence of His life and doctrine."

In two thousand years of literary production, no author or group of authors has been able to produce a character so perfect as that of Jesus. No other author or group of authors writing fact or fiction has been able to produce a worthy comparison to Jesus' unique perfection as portrayed in the four Gospels.

How was this portrait of perfection produced? What was the source? Who—individual or group—who could author such perfection?

This problem presents the skeptic with a dilemma: *one*, he must accept the portrayal of Jesus' perfection in the New Testament as a true record of an actual person or, *two*, he must find or produce a reasonable source or sources that could have produced this portrayal of perfection. History provides no such source. In two thousand years, neither the best of humanity nor the imagination of literary genius has been able to produce a competitor for the perfection which Jesus lived. Jesus was and remains unique.

The New Testament is what it claims to be, the Word of God. The authors of the New Testament simply recorded what they heard and saw and remembered. This required no special literary ability, theological understanding, or philosophical insight. The New Testament writers did not invent or imagine Jesus' perfection. Such a concept was beyond their ability to invent, imagine, or improve— as it has been beyond the ability of any person or persons to duplicate or to improve for two thousand years.

A study of literature refutes a skeptic's supposition that an unknown group of editors took the simple story of a very human Jesus and created this matchless portrait. Two reasons make the supposition of an embellished record of Jesus unacceptable: *one*, history has no knowledge of any single writer or group of writers capable of creating this perfection; *two*, reason declares such editing to be psychologically impossible. If editors or writers could have collaborated to create a fiction with Jesus' perfection, such editors and writers would themselves present a problem impossible to solve.

On the one hand, these editors and writers would have the spiritual insight to create the perfect God-man and, at the same time, these editors or writers would have the satanic malice to create the supreme blasphemy against God and the supreme deceit for mankind. Such a combination is psychologically impossible.

Philip Schaff declared, "A character so original, so complete, so uniformly consistent, so perfect, so human, and yet so high above all human greatness, can be neither a fraud nor a fiction. The poet, as has been well said, would in this case be greater than the hero. It would take more than a Jesus to invent a Jesus."

The explanation stands firm that the Gospel writers simply recorded what they had seen and heard as their memory was assisted by the Holy Spirit. The Gospels are true historical records of their actual memories of Jesus as they were assisted by the Spirit of God. This is what Jesus promised! This is what took place!

The facts vindicate the Bible record.

CHAPTER TWELVE

The Sixth Test Continued:
Reality #3. Jesus Accepted Worship as God

The integrity of the Gospel portrait of Jesus must demonstrate truth in the response Jesus gave to what people said about him. How did Jesus respond to the affirmations of his disciples? How did Jesus respond to those who worshiped him as God? How Jesus responded to those who believed he was God is an inescapable test of the integrity of his character.

Consider these recorded examples of Jesus' response to individual affirmations because they give indisputable evidence that he accepted worship as deity, showing it to be the correct and rightful human response.

1. Jesus' response to Simon Peter. Jesus deliberately asked his disciples to affirm verbally their opinion of his identity. Matthew gives a clear record of the conversation:

When Jesus came to the region of Caesarea Philippi, he asked his disciples, "Who do people say the Son of Man is?"

They replied, "Some say John the Baptist; others say Elijah; and still others, Jeremiah or one of the prophets."

"But what about you?" he asked. "Who do you say I am?"

Simon Peter answered, "You are the Christ, the Son of the living God."

Exactly what Peter meant by "Son of the living God" may be disputed, but at the very least it implies a supernatural relationship to the God revealed throughout the Old Testament and worshiped as supreme. And how did Jesus respond? Jesus not only accepted the affirmation as correct but blessed Peter for his statement. If Jesus did not believe that Peter's affirmation was correct, then Jesus' response encouraged Peter in a blasphemy.

Jesus replied, "Blessed are you, Simon son of Jonah, for this was not revealed to you by man, but by my Father in heaven" (Matthew 16:16).

Consider the inescapable facts established by this conversation. It is a fact that the liberal theologian can read this conversation and declare,"It was Peter who asserted that Jesus was the Messiah. Jesus himself did not initiate the claim to be God's unique representative."

It is also a fact that Jesus' response did not correct Simon Peter. Instead, Jesus confirmed Peter's affirmation as true by asserting that his heavenly Father had revealed this truth to Peter.

2. Jesus' response to the Samaritan woman. When Jesus talked with the Samaritan woman, the conversation concluded as follows:

The woman said, "I know that Messiah" (called Christ) "is coming. When he comes, he will explain everything to us." Then Jesus declared, "I who speak to you am he" (John 4:25–26).

Jesus' response to the woman, combined with the later Samaritan affirmation that he, Jesus, was the Savior of the world (verse 42), compels the conclusion that Jesus consciously and deliberately accepted their affirmation of him as the divine Savior.

3. Jesus' response to the man born blind. The New Testament record declares that Jesus gave sight to a man born blind. John's Gospel declares that Jesus accepted worship from the man.

Jesus heard that they had thrown him out, and when he found him, he said, "Do you believe in the Son of Man?"

"Who is he, sir?" the man asked. "Tell me so that I may believe in him."

Jesus said, "You have now seen him; in fact, he is the one speaking with you."

Then the man said, "Lord, I believe," and he worshiped him (John 9:35–38).

In this conversation Jesus claimed to be the Son of Man, a title signifying Messiahship. And Jesus accepted his unhesitating faith-filled worship. Some may argue that this was only "religious veneration"—like some people today offer to saints. Perhaps. But the Greek word *proskuneo*, used here, is the same word found in

Matthew 4:10, where Jesus declares, "Worship [*proskuneo*] the Lord your God, and serve him only." And Jesus accepted this man's believing "worship."

4. Jesus' response to the high priest. In Mark's record of the predawn trial of Jesus, Jesus gives an unequivocal response to the question by the high priest.

Again the high priest asked him, "Are you the Christ, the Son of the Blessed One?"

"I am," said Jesus. "And you will see the Son of Man sitting at the right hand the Mighty One and coming on the clouds of heaven" (Mark 14:61–62).

The high priest immediately declared that Jesus' statement was blasphemy. The high priest would have been correct if Jesus was only a man. Jesus' statement to the high priest allows no interpretation other than that Jesus claimed to be God's unique Son. His reply can be understood only as a claim of deity, even though he knew that his claim meant his death.

5. Jesus' response to Thomas. To the doubting Thomas, Jesus challenged,

"Put your finger here; see my hands. Reach out your hand and put it into my side. Stop doubting and believe."

Thomas said to him, "My Lord and my God" (John 20:27–28).

Remember that Thomas was a monotheistic Jew who believed in only one God. He here confessed that Jesus was that God. And Jesus accepted from his apostle the adoration and worship that belongs only to God.

These five responses, chosen from many similar assertions made by Jesus to his contemporaries, require a reasonable decision from three alternatives:

1. Jesus knew that he was actually the Son of the living God. In his teachings and responses he was teaching people to believe his true identity and to worship him as deity. It is true that Jesus and the Father are One. His deity merits human worship.

2. Jesus honestly believed that he was the Son of God although he was only human. He was deluded and was teaching his followers

to share his delusion. In short, Jesus was crazed and deserves our pity instead of our worship. The Christian faith is based upon delusion and should be rejected.

3. Jesus knew he was not the Son of God. He deliberately deceived his followers and commissioned them to propagate a lie. Jesus was a devilish deceiver and a blasphemer. His contemporaries were correct in putting him to death and in trying to stop the deception. The Christian faith is built on the world's greatest deception and should be rejected.

Only one of the three statements can state the truth! Fair judgment must choose between three alternatives. And only one choice can be correct.

Choice One. Jesus was good. Jesus was truly God revealing himself to mankind and receiving the worship proper to deity, *or,*

Choice Two. Jesus was crazed. Jesus was deluded and, therefore, at least partly insane. Jesus was himself deceived in believing in his deity and was deluding others into the same error, *or,*

Choice Three. Jesus was evil. Though Jesus knew that he was only human, he sought deliberately to deceive others into believing that he was God.

Only one choice can be correct!

In *C. S. Lewis Through the Shadowlands*, Brian Shelby, director of the Christian Arts Center Group, describes how the renowned English scholar viewed the inescapable alternatives:

The red studio light is switched on. The BBC announcer tells listeners that Mr. C. S. Lewis is about to give the third of five talks on "What Christians Believe." The green cue light flashes and the man at the microphone begins to speak.

For the next quarter of an hour he booms at the microphone in a voice that has been described as sounding like a cannonade at sea. He attacks the ether, bombards the listener with his thoughts and ideas.

". . . There suddenly turns up a man who goes about talking as if He was God. He claims to forgive sins. He says He has always existed. He says He is coming to judge the world at the end of time. Now let us get this clear . . . I'm trying here to prevent anyone from saying the really silly things that people say about Him: 'I'm ready to accept Jesus as a great moral teacher, but I don't accept His claim to be God.' That's the one thing we mustn't say. A man who was merely a man and said the sort of things Jesus said wouldn't be a great moral teacher! He'd either be a lunatic—on a level with the man who says he's a poached egg—or else he'd be the Devil of Hell.

"You must make your choice. Either this man was, and is, the Son of God: or else a madman or something worse. You can shut Him up for a fool; you can spit at Him and kill Him as a demon; or you can fall at His feet and call Him Lord and God. But don't let us come with any patronizing nonsense about His being a 'great human teacher.' He hasn't left that open to us. He didn't intend to."

The choice is clear and limited.

CHAPTER THIRTEEN

The Sixth Test Continued:
Reality # 4. Jesus Claimed to Be God

The integrity of the Gospel portrait must demonstrate truth not only in Jesus's responses to affirmations by others but also in his own claims about himself. Jesus must claim no more or no less than his true relationship with deity and with humanity.

What were Jesus' claims? How did his hearers understand these claims? Did Jesus teach the truth about himself? Four affirmations by Jesus adequately demonstrate his practice. In unequivocal clarity Jesus repeatedly claimed to be God with the ability to forgive sin and to give eternal life to believers.

Climaxing his claim to be the bread of life, Jesus declared that he had deity power to bestow eternal life, saying, *"I tell you the truth, he who believes has everlasting life. I am the bread of life"* (John 6:47–48).

Jesus emphasized that his deity ability to save by giving eternal life was unique and exclusive by saying, *"I tell you the truth. I am the gate for the sheep. All who ever came before me were thieves and robbers, but the sheep did not listen to them. I am the gate; whoever enters through me will be saved. He will come in and go out, and find pasture. . . . My sheep listen to my voice; I know them, and they follow me. I give them eternal life; and they shall never perish; no one can snatch them out of my hand"* (John 10:7–9, 27–28).

By these statements Jesus not only claimed authority as God to save those who come to him for eternal life but he condemned all others who claimed to be saviors as thieves and deceivers.

To his disciples Jesus was even more specific in his deity claim to exclusive ability to save, saying, *"I am the way and the truth and the life. No one comes to the Father except through me"* (John 14:6). Jesus claimed unique power. Jesus claimed an exclusive relationship with the Father as the ONLY way, truth, or life. Jesus claimed the power of deity.

Just before Jesus resurrected Lazarus from the grave, the Jews raised the question of Jesus' identity. The conversation ended in Jesus' claim that defies misinterpretation:

Jesus said, "I and the Father are one."

Again the Jews picked up stones to stone him, but Jesus said to them, "I have shown you many great miracles from the Father. For which of these do you stone me?"

"We are not stoning you for any of these," replied the Jews, "but for blasphemy, because you, a mere man, claim to be God" (John 10:32–33).

This conversation allows only one conclusion: Jesus claimed identity with God. Jesus' hearers accused Him of blasphemy because they understood that he was claiming to be God. Jesus' claim leaves an inescapable choice! If Jesus' claim to be God was false, he was guilty of blasphemy; if Jesus' claim to be God was true, the Jews were guilty of rejecting God's Son come in the flesh.

In John's record of Jesus' high priestly prayer, Jesus specifies that his unique power to save rests upon a unique relationship to the Father: *"For you granted him authority over all people that he might give eternal life to all those you have given him. Now this is life eternal: that they may know you, the only true God, and Jesus Christ, whom you have sent"* (John 17:2–3).

These few samples afford sufficient evidence to enable fair judgment to choose between three possible alternatives. Only one alternative can be correct. The choice is inescapable!

Choice One: Jesus was good. Jesus was truly God declaring his deity to mankind as the ONLY Savior for lost humanity, *or,*

Choice Two: Jesus was crazed. Jesus was deluded and, therefore, at least partly insane. Jesus was deceived himself and was deluding others into a false hope about his power to save the lost, *or,*

Choice Three: Jesus was evil. Though Jesus knew that he was only human, he sought deliberately to deceive others into believing that he was God come in the flesh and, therefore, the only Savior for a lost humanity.

Only one choice can be correct!

Either Jesus spoke the truth about himself when he said that he and the Father were one or the crucifiers were right when they said, "He is a blasphemer."

Jesus cannot be a liar and also be a good teacher.

Jesus cannot be crazed and also be an authentic prophet.

Jesus cannot be a deceiver and also be a good man.

Henck Johnson was stating the only reasonable judgment when he declared: "Christ was either the grandest, guiltiest of imposters, by a marvelous and most subtle refinement of wickedness, or He was God manifest in the flesh."

Dr. Augustus Strong, author of the classic Baptist *Systematic Theology*, made this inescapable assessment: "For Confucius or Buddha, Zoroaster or Pythagoras, Socrates or Mohammed to claim all power in heaven and earth, would show insanity or moral perversion. But that is exactly what Jesus claimed. He was either mentally or morally unsound, or his testimony is true."

Great scholars see that the choice is inescapable! Great scholars see that only one choice is reasonable! Jesus is the Son of God!

And because the testimony of Jesus stands true, the validity of the Bible stands equally true—because Jesus declared: *"Do not think that I have come to abolish the Law or the Prophets; I have not come to abolish them but to fulfill them. I tell you the truth, until heaven and earth disappear, not the smallest letter, not the least stroke of a pen, will by any means disappear from the Law until everything is accomplished"* (Matthew 5:17–18).

CHAPTER FOURTEEN

Inward Evidence of the Validity of the Gospels

Although it may seem redundant and repetitious, let us reconsider the validity of the Gospel record as a whole in its presentation of Jesus. Skeptics have attempted to separate the figure of Jesus as presented in the Gospels into two segments: one, the actual historical figure of Jesus; two, the embellished figure of Jesus. According to their reasoning, the actual historical Jesus was just a man and the Gospel Jesus is a gradual embellishment. Try to imagine a possible procedure to account for such an embellishment. Four simple men write their personal and/or collected memories of Jesus. Though each one's record is slightly different in parts, they achieve basic unity. There is no contradiction. After this, unknown writers add occasional complimentary but falsified or imagined embellishments to the initial compositions. Is it possible to imagine that the cumulative result would attain the universally recognized perfection of the Gospel picture of Jesus?

Since the Gospels have been completed, recognized scholars have tried to eliminate the supposed embellishments and construct a more accurate portrait of Christ. Lack of agreement as to these imaginative projections among such scholars emphasizes the difficulty, if not the impossibility, of making a "corrected" identity. Time and sound scholarship have rejected every such attempt to diminish the perfection set forth in the Gospel presentation of Jesus.

To the Bible-believing layperson who is unwilling to swap fact for fanciful theory, these imaginary explanations for the Gospels meet immediate rejection as unreasonable, even ridiculous. Only a person bent on rejecting the Bible could take refuge in such contrived explanations that seek to justify unbelief.

Time-tested Biblical scholarship has presented a simpler and more reasonable scenario, one which the average layperson can understand. Sound scholarship recognizes that discovering the historical and actual portrait of Jesus affords only a few reasonable alternatives. The only two possibilities are so simple that even the most uneducated can follow to certainty.

First possibility: The New Testament record of Jesus is entirely true and unembellished. The Gospel writers simply wrote what they and other disciples remembered as guided by the Holy Spirit. Different personalities and purposes account for the variations in the Gospel records; the aid and guidance of the Holy Spirit account for their unity. Moreover, without the aid of the Holy Spirit, as promised by Jesus, human slips and errors would have prevented the unity in the Gospels.

The only other possibility: The New Testament record of Jesus is partly true and partly embellished. Some persons, who are completely unknown in history, began to add to the initial Gospel record in order to make a more exalted Christ. By some unimaginable process these false additions gradually but finally produced the perfection of the New Testament portrait of Jesus.

Consider what the choice between these two possibilities requires.

First, if the New Testament record of Jesus is true and unembellished, valid and accurate, then the explanation is plausible that the Gospel writers simply wrote what they or contemporary eyewitnesses saw, heard, and remembered. Three years of ministry by the Son of God could provide even poor memories with ample materials under the promised Holy Spirit's guidance. Writing the true record of the life of Jesus would be possible and reasonable because the writers were simply recording eyewitness memories with the guidance of the promised Holy Spirit.

Second, if the New Testament record presents an embellished and falsified picture of Jesus, then fair judgment cannot escape the following problems:

First, the person or persons who wrote the embellished additions to the portrait of the historical Jesus would necessarily have to possess incredible biographical skill. Why is this a difficulty?

Because no scholar or school of scholars is known to have arisen in two thousand years who has been capable of separating the actual Jesus from the embellished Jesus. Secondly, because no intellectual scholar or imaginative writer has arisen in two thousand years who has been capable of improving the Gospel portrait of Jesus. It is ridiculous to imagine that the unschooled apostles or subsequent believers were capable of fabricating just the necessary but false embellishments to create this perfection. Nor does history set forth any literary person or persons having the genius to fabricate a portrait of Jesus so perfect that two thousand years of prolific writers has produced no equal.

Moreover, the person or persons who could compose the false, embellished portrait of the historical Jesus would necessarily have to possess the highest ethical and spiritual concepts, because no saint or scholar has arisen in two thousand years who has been capable of duplicating or surpassing their creation. At the same time, the person or persons who could compose the false, embellished portrait of the historical Jesus would have to possess such an evil nature that he, she or they would deliberately invent and communicate the supreme deceit of history. Why is this true? Because he, she or they would be concocting a deceit that promised eternal salvation on the basis of a fiction which they had deliberately and deceitfully written.

Honest scholarship must accept the fact that two thousand years of history knows of no writer or group of writers, ethical or wicked, sincere or deceptive, who were capable of inventing and producing such an unrivaled masterpiece of perfection as the Gospel portrait of Jesus.

A recognized psychological principle declares that it is impossible for a person or persons to have the satanic nature capable of inventing and producing such deceit and at the same time have the genius to conceive and produce the portrait of a person of such ethical and spiritual perfection that no equal has been produced in sacred or secular literature for the past two millennia.

The alternatives for a reasonable explanation for the validity of the New Testament Gospels are limited and inescapable:

1. The New Testament is a book written with the intent of deliberate and satanic deceit, *or,*

2. The New Testament is a book written by writers who were religiously deluded but at the same time possessed an ethical perception of moral perfection and the genius to portray it in writing, *or,*

3. The New Testament is a book with a base of truth that has been embellished by unknown writers with unknown motivations, *or,*

4. The New Testament is a book of truth written by the disciples of Jesus who simply told what eyewitnesses had seen and heard as the Holy Spirit of God aided their memories.

The choice is limited to these four and is logically inescapable!

Rudolph Kogel clearly stated the only reasonable decision that each person must make, saying: "If the Holy Scriptures are God's word, then submit to it, body and soul. Upon this rock you must build your houses as against storms and tempests; upon this rock you must build your churches as against the gates of hell. If, however, it be nothing more than a book full of superstition and chimerical fancies, or fantastical delusions or antiquated notions, then prohibit its entrance into your houses and schools."

Fair judgment cannot accept either the explanation that the New Testament is a book of deliberate deceit or an imaginative attempt to embellish the figure of the Son of God with fabrications. And, of course, the final blow to the theory of embellishment is the fact that the earliest Gospel manuscripts and versions agree with the contemporary versions.

Fair judgment and inescapable facts validate the truth of the New Testament Gospel records!

CHAPTER FIFTEEN

Additional Confirmation:
The Cultural Effects of the Bible

All books, but more especially all sacred books, must face the test of the good or bad effects that they have exerted upon the cultures of their adherents. To deny that books have power to affect culture is unrealistic. No study of India can ignore the cultural effects of the Hindu religion. The teachings of Buddha have created and preserved cultural patterns affecting every facet of life in China and the Koreas. Taoism and emperor worship dominated Japanese culture for centuries. The Koran continues to mold the culture of Iraq and Iran. It is an indisputable fact that the Bible has influenced the cultures of most of Europe and all of the Americas. Though the degree of influence varies, who would dispute the fact that religious books do affect even secular society? For this reason the Bible, like other sacred books, must face the test of its effect upon the culture of its adherents.

The Bible welcomes this very practical test!

Some enemies of the Bible have unfairly condemned the Bible and the Christian church on the basis of the evils of the Inquisition. While we concede that leaders who professed faith in Christ and the Bible committed this inhuman persecution, fair judgment will show that this admitted cruelty was contrary to the teaching of Christ and the Bible. This cruelty arose from man's misuse of secular and ecclesiastical authority. The teachings of Jesus clearly condemn all cruelty and persecution. The evil of the Inquisition was not produced by the Bible or by Christian faith, but rather by a worldly and evil— even though ecclesiastical—human organizational power structure.

Valid judgment of the Bible must rest on the following evidences: *one*, the written and considered evaluation by historically recognized molders of culture; *two*, the comparative status of human rights, opportunities, and liberties where the Bible is taught with areas where the Bible is not taught.

1. *Evaluation of the Bible's significance by historically recognized leaders whose works have influenced culture.*

First, consider the observations of philosophers who have greatly influenced modern education and culture. No one questions the place of Francis Bacon, English philosopher of the 16th and 17th centuries. He said, "There was never found, in any age of the world, either religion or law that did so highly exalt the public good as the Bible." In the next century, the English philosopher John Locke declared, "In morality there are books enough written by ancient and modern philosophers, but the morality of the Gospel doth so exceed them all that to give a man a full knowledge of true morality I shall send him to no other book than the New Testament."

Even the renowned eighteenth century German philosopher Immanuel Kant declared, "The existence of the Bible is the greatest blessing which humanity has ever experienced."

In the nineteenth century, the famous biologist Thomas Henry Huxley, though an agnostic, stated that the Bible is "the Magna Carta of the poor and the oppressed." Huxley even argued for the reading of the Bible in schools, saying, "By the study of what other book could children be so humanized, and made to feel that each figure in that vast historical procession fills, like themselves, but a momentary space in the interval between two eternities, and earns the blessings or the curses of all times, according to its effort to do good and to hate evil, even as they are earning their payment for their work?"

Poets, authors, and political figures often express the true convictions of the culture in which they live. In the eighteenth and nineteenth century Samuel Coleridge said, "For more than a thousand years the Bible, collectively taken, has gone hand in hand with civilization, science, law; in short, with the moral and intellectual cultivation of the species, always supporting and often leading the way." Samuel Johnson, eighteenth century lexicographer and author, was impressed by the number of great men in history who have accepted the truth of the Bible, saying, "As to the Christian religion, besides the strong evidence which we have for it, there is a balance in its favor from the number of great men who have been convinced of its truth after a serious consideration of the question. Sir Isaac Newton set out an infidel, and came to be a very firm believer."

Affirmations of faith in the Bible by political greats make the proper choice for inclusion difficult, but here are three that impress me. Admirers of Benjamin Franklin cannot omit his statement: "As to Jesus of Nazareth, my opinion of whom you particularly desire, I think the system of morals and his religion, as he left them to us, is the best the world ever saw, or is likely to see." Then consider the incident from an honored soldier, Andrew Jackson, who, pointing to the Bible, said to a friend, "That book, sir, is the rock on which our republic stands." And from the same period in United States history, William H. Seward, Secretary of State, declared: "I do not believe human society, including not merely a few persons in any state, but the whole masses of men, ever has attained, or ever can attain, a high state of intelligence, virtue, security, liberty, or happiness, without the Holy Scriptures."

Historians who have earned continuing recognition for accuracy in their record of events and movements have stated their evaluation of the Bible and its cultural effects. W. H. Lecky declared that "the great characteristic of Christianity, and the moral proof of its divinity, is that it has been the main source of the moral development of Europe, and that it has discharged this office not so much by the inclination of a system of ethics, however pure, as by the assimilating and attractive influence of a perfect ideal. The moral progress of mankind can never cease to be distinctively and intensely Christian as long as it consists of a gradual approximation of the character of the Christian Founder."

Though not recognized as a Christian, H. G. Wells wrote, "The Bible has been the Book that held together the fabric of Western civilization. It has been the handbook of life to countless millions of men and women. The civilization we possess could not have come into existence and could not have been sustained without it."

Is it any wonder, therefore, that a scholar who was respected on two continents, James Orr, professor at the United Free Church College, Glasgow, Scotland, should conclude, "In national life the Bible is the source of our highest social and national aspirations."

Mary Ellen Chase, distinguished novelist and professor of English Literature at Smith College, declared, "The language of the Bible, now simple and direct in its homely vigor, now sonorous and stately in its richness, has placed an indelible stamp upon our best writers from Bacon to Lincoln and even to the present day. Without it there would be no *Paradise Lost*, no *Samson Agonistes*, no *Pilgrim's Progress*; no William Blake, or Whittier, or T. S. Eliot as we know them; no Emerson or Thoreau, no Negro Spirituals, no Address at Gettysburg. Without it the words of Burke and Washington, Patrick Henry and Winston Churchill would miss their eloquence and their meaning."

William Lyon Phelps, an academic giant, said, "I thoroughly believe in a university education for both men and women; but I believe a knowledge of the Bible without a college course is more valuable than a college course without the Bible."

No other book, secular or sacred, ancient or modern, has ever contributed the cultural benefits to as many nations and races as the Bible. No other book competes with the Bible's unique record.

2. *A comparison of human rights, opportunities, and liberties where the Bible is taught with areas where the Bible is not taught.*

If a person were to place a map of the geographical and political regions influenced by the Bible over a map of the world, what would it teach us about the influence of the Bible on human rights, opportunities, and liberties? It would reveal that those countries in which women and children have rights, in which governments practice social justice and in which civil and personal liberty is enjoyed, are the geographical and political areas in which the Bible and the faith it reveals has been proclaimed.

This test was confirmed by the decision in the case of *Updegraph v. Commonwealth*, 1826, when this judicial opinion was stated: "No free government now exists except where Christianity is acknowledged, and is the religion of the country." History has failed to disprove the challenge made in 1906 by the renowned scholar

Dr. A. H. Strong, in his classic *Systematic Theology*, saying, "When the microscopic search of skepticism, which has hunted the heavens and sounded the seas to disprove the existence of a Creator, has turned its attention to human society and has found on this planet a place ten miles square where a decent man can live in decency, comfort, and security, supporting and educating his children, unspoiled and unpolluted; a place where age is reverenced, infancy protected, manhood respected, womanhood honored, and human life held in due regard—when skeptics can find such a place ten miles square on this globe, where the gospel of Christ has not gone and cleared the way and laid the foundations and made decency and security possible, it will then be in order for the skeptical literati to move thither and ventilate their views."

The reverse side of these factual declarations explains the rapid increase in violence, sexual immorality, suicide and murder, physical and sexual abuse of women and children since the Bible has been removed from the public schools in the United States.

Fair judgment rejects the materialistic explanation that these Biblical cultural benefits result from an accidental coincidence of sociological advance.

Fair judgment will accept ONLY the explanation that the social and ethical standards of the Bible have caused the social and cultural benefits in Christian civilizations. The cultural benefits of the contents of the Bible add evidence that validates the Bible.

CHAPTER SIXTEEN

Still Another Confirmation: Scholars and Scientists

From the time of its infancy in Jerusalem, the Christian church has endured attack. Political and physical persecution failed, however, to stop or even slow the first missionaries and the rapid increase of converts. By A.D. 395 the formerly persecuted church dominated the Roman Empire so that Theodosius the Great decreed Christianity to be the established religion of Rome. Political and physical persecution had proved futile against the church.

With political and social acceptance, the church began to face the attacks of internal division, worldliness, heresy, and false religions. Gnosticism, Manichaeanism, Montanism, and the invasion of pagan religions caused thoughtful leaders to lead the church to growing clarity in its doctrine concerning Christ and the Bible. As physical persecution had failed, so intellectual challenge met defeat. Faith in the Bible as God's Word grew more established.

During the Dark Ages the scholars of the Christian church were the keepers of the light of learning. The best minds of the Eastern and Western cultures grew in their understanding of Biblical doctrines and their faith in the validity of the Bible.

As the light grew into the fifteenth century, reformers such as Savonarola and Jan Hus began to denounce the corruption of the church . . . but the validity of the Bible stood firm. The sixteenth century responded to the courage of Martin Luther, John Calvin, and the Mennonites. Great minds challenged the authority of the institutional church by exalting the authority of the Bible.

The eighteenth century witnessed both the benefits of Wesley's fidelity to the Bible and the horrors of the "blood bath" of the French departure from the Bible. Both the Biblical revival in England and the atheistic revolution in France gave proof in varied ways of the value and validity of the Bible.

The point in this brief review of history focuses upon the fact that the best minds in history have recognized the Bible's authenticity.

Time has produced two types of thinkers: the temporary and the timeless. The temporary are like Roman candles, producing quick and sparkling light that fades into darkness. The timeless are like stars whose light time cannot dim. Both of these schools of thinkers have evaluated the validity of the Bible. In fact, the Bible ranks as the most scrutinized, analyzed, assessed, evaluated, and tested book of all time. Dr. Henry Morris, President Emeritus of the Institute for Creation Research, which has a membership of over 700 scientists with postgraduate degrees in a pure or applied natural science, summarizes the verdict of the history of scholarly evaluation of the Bible, saying, "The Bible has stood the test of the most searching scientific investigations and has emerged stronger than ever."

To confirm the fact that the indisputable leaders in the field of intellectual accomplishments and of scientific development have recognized and asserted the validity and integrity of the Bible, I have collected a few of the published evaluations of the Bible by historically recognized intellectuals. I will quote only the evaluation about the validity of the Bible that is given by timeless thinkers, many in the field of the physical sciences.

Francis Bacon (1561–1626), Lord Chancellor of England, stated, "There are two books laid before us to study, to prevent our falling into error; first the volume of the Scriptures, which reveal the will of God; then the volume of the Creatures, which express His power."

Isaac Newton, the discoverer of the universal law of gravitation and the formulator of the three laws of motion which made possible the discipline of dynamics, expressed his belief in the validity of the Bible by saying, "We account the Scriptures of God to be the most sublime philosophy. I find more sure marks of authenticity in the Bible than in any profane history whatsoever."

Michael Faraday, one of the greatest physicists of all time and inventor of the generator, declared, "The Bible, and it alone, with nothing added to it nor taken away from it by man, is the sole and sufficient guide for each individual, at all times and in all circumstances. . . . Faith in the divinity and work of Christ is the gift of God, and the evidence of this faith is obedience to the commandment of Christ."

John Herschel, the outstanding astronomer who discovered 500 new nebulae and cataloged the stars and nebulae of both the northern and southern hemispheres, said, "All human discoveries seem to be made only for the purpose of confirming more and more strongly the truths that come from on high and are contained in the sacred writings."

Samuel F.B. Morse, inventor of the telegraph and a famous artist, expressed his growing faith in the integrity of the Bible by this confession: "The nearer I approach to the end of my pilgrimage, the clearer is the evidence of the divine origin of the Bible, the grandeur and sublimity of God's remedy for fallen man are more appreciated, and the future is illumined with hope and joy."

James Dana, Yale professor and President of the Geological Society of America and the American Association for the Advancement of Science, declared his evaluation of the Bible by saying: "The grand old Book of God still stands; and this old earth, the more its leaves are turned over and pondered, the more it will sustain and illustrate the sacred Word."

Joseph Lister, the English surgeon who developed antiseptic surgery through the use of chemical disinfectants and the president of the Royal Society and the British Association, declared his faith by saying, "I am a believer in the fundamental doctrines of Christianity."

In 1864 an official statement affirming confidence in the scientific integrity of the Holy Scriptures and known as *The Declaration of Students of the Natural and Physical Sciences* was issued in London and signed by 717 scientists.

Alexander MacAlister, professor of Anatomy at Cambridge and author of books on zoology and physiology, wrote a revealing evaluation of the skeptics of the Bible, saying, "I think the widespread impression of the agnosticism of scientific men is largely due to the attitude taken up by a few of the past popularizers of science, like Tyndall and Huxley. It has been my experience that the disbelief in the revelation that God has given in the life and work, death and resurrection of our Savior is more prevalent among what I may call the camp followers of science than amongst those to whom scientific work is the business of their lives."

Since the first century and through the nineteenth century, famed scholars have been earnest Christians. For almost two thousand years a multitude of recognized intellects have been part and parcel with the Christian faith. These scholars were staunch defenders of the integrity of the Bible and the deity of Jesus Christ.

Even during the twentieth century, when the academic world has become increasingly secularized, Christian scholarship has continued to thrive. Yet no school of academic thought, even those with atheistic and materialistic philosophies, has been able to bring any accusation against the validity of the Bible or the deity of the Christ that has weathered the test of fact and time. The hammers of opposition wear out; the Bible anvil continues to stand strong.

The voyage of Columbus proved that the world was round and not flat. The experiments of Pasteur proved that life is not spontaneously generated. Scientific error has not been able to stand against the barrage of investigation during the Christian era . . . but the validity of the Bible has stood every test.

Fair judgment and common sense cannot accept the explanation that the Christian faith in the validity of the Bible continues because adequate scholarship has made no investigation.

Fair judgment cannot accept the explanation that no scholar of adequate stature has arisen to challenge the validity of the Bible and of Jesus as the Son of God.

Fair judgment can accept only the explanation that the greatest minds of the centuries have been compelled by the facts and constant study to confirm the church's faith in the validity of the Bible and the deity of Jesus.

Now that you have read what these time-tested "thinkers" have said about the validity of the Bible, I will ask you only two questions:

1. Do you honestly think that you have made an adequate study of the Bible to justify your denial of the validity of the Bible when these timeless thinkers have spoken so clearly of their faith?

2. Do you honestly think that you have made a fair and honest assessment of the place that the Bible should have in your own life?

CHAPTER SEVENTEEN

The Bible's Challenge and
Man's Inescapable Decision

The Bible challenges every person with an uncompromising choice about eternal salvation. The Bible claims to be the *unique* source of the self-revelation of the true God. The Bible insists that no other book or writing can deserve the title: THE WORD OF GOD.

The Bible claims to reveal the only true way of eternal salvation. And the fact is that no other religion offers forgiveness of sins and eternal life. All other religions are self-effort rituals with not even a promise of redemptive grace. The Bible offers the one and only true hope for man's eternal salvation. No other religion claims God's redemptive sacrifice or resurrection power.

This exclusive claim faces every person with the challenge of an inescapable choice: Personally trust the Bible's God, the Bible's plan of salvation and be eternally saved; refuse to trust the Bible's God and the Bible's plan of salvation, or choose any variation, and be eternally lost.

The Bible permits no compromise or alternative. Dryden expressed it as follows:

> *Whence but from Heaven, could men unskill'd in arts,*
> *In several ages born, in several parts,*
> *Weave such agreeing truths? or how, or why*
> *Should all conspire to cheat us with a lie?*

Because the Bible is the only inspired source of spiritual truth concerning God's gracious plan of redemption, every person is faced with an inescapable choice: Obey what the Bible teaches and be saved; reject or neglect what the Bible teaches and be lost.

The Bible claim allows no alternative or compromise!

The only justification for this inescapable choice is what this book has stated:

The Bible is what it claims to be: the Word of God. The best evidence for this unique claim is the Bible itself. As Charles Hodge, the classic Princeton theologian, stated: "The best evidence of the Bible's being the word of God is to be found between its pages. It proves itself."

No religion, philosophy, educator, reformer, individual or group has been able to imagine, invent, or communicate a revelation of God and redemption that compares to the Bible. Not in the Orient nor the West, not among philosophers or theologians, not among mystics or visionaries has it been accomplished. The Bible claim remains true: Man by his wisdom knew not God; man by his wisdom has not been able to invent a system of gracious salvation that compares with that of the Bible.

Truly, fair judgment will permit only one reasonable explanation: The Bible is what it claims to be: the Word of God!

The Common-Sense Judgmental Conclusion

These simple tests—size, unity, accuracy, prophecy, quality of message, personification of perfection, cultural effect, scholarly acceptance—demonstrate the distinctives in the Bible's self-proof. When the skeptic rejects the believer's testimony of inward assurance, the believer has no sufficient means for overcoming the rejection; when the skeptic rejects the scholar's rational philosophical arguments, the scholar has no tangible or sure way of refuting the rejection. *But the Bible's self-proof differs.* For the skeptic to continue in his rejection of the Bible, he faces the challenge to give a reasonable explanation for the unique characteristics of the Bible. The Bible as an objective and tangible object raises an inescapable factual challenge that demands a reasonable explanation.

Fair judgment requires that the skeptic must discover some adequate and reasonable explanation for the unique qualities of the Bible and provide reasonable answers to the objective challenge of its contents.

Flippant or considered denial instead of factual explanation fails to answer the challenge.

The Bible challenges the honesty, wisdom, and faith of every man!

The Inescapable Decision

The Bible, vindicated by facts, offers salvation to all who will "believe on the Lord Jesus Christ" (Acts 16:30–31). This unique personal salvation provides both a present divine help and a future eternal home.

The uncertainty of life combines with the certainty of death to challenge each person with an inescapable decision: What will you do with Jesus?

How can any reasonable person refuse, postpone, or delay the personal acceptance of God's gracious offer to forgive your sins, to give you eternal life?

Facts have demonstrated by reasonable tests that the Bible is the Word of God!

Facts have demonstrated that Jesus is sinful man's only Savior and Lord!

Your only wise choice: "I believe what the Bible teaches. I now repent of my sins and place my complete trust in Jesus Christ as my Savior and Lord."

WHAT IS YOUR DECISION?

Wise indeed is the person who prays the following prayer and receives God's gracious answer.

Dear Lord Jesus,

I know that I am a sinner and need Your forgiveness. I believe that You died for my sins. I want to turn from my sins. I now invite You to come into my heart and life. I want to trust and follow You as Lord and Savior. By faith I now receive You into my heart and life and believe that You forgive my sins and give me life. I thank You for saving me. Amen.

Welcome home!

Part Two:
Evidence Confirmed—

Recognized Leaders Testify

*If leaders who receive world recognition are willing to
publically state their faith in the Bible as the Word of God,
how can you glibly deny the validity of the Bible?*

Dr. Henry M. Morris

A Leading Scientist Looks at the Bible

Hundreds of books have been written on the subject of the divine inspiration of the Bible, and the evidences for it are many and varied. If one will seriously investigate these Biblical and scientific evidences, he will find the claims of its inspiration are amply justified.

One case in point is the remarkable attestation of fulfilled prophecy. For example, look at Daniel 9:24–27. In about 538 B.C., Daniel the prophet predicted that the Anointed One—the Messiah— would come as Israel's Savior and Prince 483 years after the Persian emperor would give the Jews authority to rebuild Jerusalem, which was then in ruins. This was clearly and definitely fulfilled hundreds of years later. This is but one of the more than 300 Old Testament prophecies that were fulfilled by Christ during the time of His first coming. Another group of prophecies (Ezekiel 37:22, Isaiah 11:11, Luke 21:24, and many others) predict the restoration of the Jews to the land of Israel as a true nation in the latter days. For almost 1500 years this seemed utterly impossible, and yet we have now seen it fulfilled in our own generation!

The historical accuracy of the Scriptures is likewise in a class by itself—far superior to the written records of Egypt, Assyria, and other early nations. Archaeological confirmations of the Biblical record have been almost innumerable in the last century. Dr. Nelson Glueck, probably the greatest modern authority on archeology in Israel, has said, "No archeological discovery has ever controverted a Biblical reference. Scores of archeological findings have been made which confirm in clear outline or in exact detail historical statements in the Bible."

Another striking evidence of divine inspiration is found in the fact that many of the principles of modern science were recorded as facts of nature in the Bible long before scientists confirmed them experimentally. A sampling of these would include the roundness of the earth (Isaiah 40:22), the almost infinite extent of the sidereal universe (Isaiah 55:9), the law of conservation of mass and energy (2 Peter 3:7), the hydrologic cycle (Ecclesiastes 1:7), the vast number of stars (Jeremiah 33:22), the equivalence of matter and energy (Hebrews 1:3), the law of increasing entropy (Psalm 102:25–27), the paramount importance of blood in life processes (Leviticus 17:11), the atmospheric circulation (Ecclesiastes 1:6), the gravitational field (Job 26:7), and many others. These are not stated in the technical jargon of modern science, of course, but in the common parlance of man's everyday experience; nevertheless, they are completely in accord with the most modern scientific facts.

The remarkable structure of the Bible should also be stressed. Although it is a collection of 66 books, written by 40 or more different men over a period of 2000 years, it is clearly one Book with perfect unity and consistency throughout.

The Bible is unique also in terms of its effect on individual men and on the history of nations. Those nations that have honored the Scriptures in their national life, God has honored and blessed.

Not one statement has ever been disproved by any real facts of science or history, and God will surely honor and bless the faith and witness of anyone who fully believes and obeys His Word.

Dr. Henry M. Morris, President Emeritus of the Institute for Creation Research, is internationally recognized as a scientist and Biblical scholar. He is the author of many books and scientific articles.

Dr. Billy Graham

A Noted Evangelist Looks at the Bible

In his autobiography, *Just As I Am,* Billy Graham tells of his personal spiritual struggle concerning the validity of the Bible as the Word of God. He emphasizes that his entire life and ministry hinged upon his decision.

Chuck Templeton, pastor of Toronto's Avenue Road Church, and Billy Graham had been close friends and companions on a whirlwind tour of the British Isles, Holland, Denmark, Belgium, and France. Templeton then resigned from his church to enroll as a graduate student at Princeton Theological Seminary. During his first year there, Templeton developed doubts concerning the authority of the Scriptures.

At the same time, Graham began to struggle with the neo-orthodoxy of such writers as Karl Barth and Reinhold Neibuhr. They challenged concepts of the Bible that Graham had held since childhood, especially the inspiration and authority of the Scriptures. Then Templeton said to Billy, "Billy, you're fifty years out of date. People no longer accept the Bible as being inspired the way you do."

The struggle reached a climax. Graham recognized that if he could not trust the Bible, he could not continue his ministry. In his distress Graham reviewed what Jesus said about the Scriptures. Then, walking alone into the night at the San Bernardino retreat, he stopped by a stump, placed his open Bible upon it and struggled in prayer with the issue.

Finally, Graham settled the issue with this prayer: "Father, I am going to accept this as Thy Word—by *faith!* I'm going to allow faith to go beyond my intellectual questions and doubts, and I will believe this to be Your inspired Word."

As an immediate confirmation, Graham declared, "I sensed the presence and power of God as I had not sensed it in months."

Following this experience, Graham testifies in work and action that God has confirmed his faith for more than half a century.

John Owen

An English Scholar Looks at the Bible

I n his *Catechism,* the eminent theologian John Owen listed seven proofs by which he indicated his belief that the Holy Spirit confirmed the Bible to be the Word of God:

1. The antiquity of the writings;
2. Their preservation from fury;
3. The prophecies in them;
4. The holiness and majesty of their doctrine agreeable to the nature of God;
5. Miracles;
6. The testimony of the church of all ages;
7. The blood of innumerable martyrs, etc.

John Calvin

A Timeless Theologian Looks at the Bible

B illy Graham's experience about the reliability of the Bible as the Word of God is but a modern example of the truth penned by John Calvin: "In vain were the authority of Scripture fortified by argument, or supported by the consent of the church, or confirmed by any other helps, if unaccompanied by an assurance higher and stronger than human judgment can give. Till this better foundation has been laid, the authority of Scripture remains in suspense. On the other hand, when recognizing its exemption from the common rule, we receive it reverently, and according to its dignity, those proofs which were not so strong as to produce and rivet a full conviction in our minds, become most appropriate helps."

True and life-molding faith springs only from the Holy Spirit because the intellect alone lacks the power to convince the reason.

Dr. Bill Bright

Founder and President of Campus Crusade for Christ International

An International Christian Leader Looks at the Bible

Many brilliant scholars have documented a wealth of irrefutable empirical evidence that the Bible is God's holy, inerrant Word, and given to us by inspiration of the Holy Spirit through its original writers.

Each individual piece of evidence is convincing; the collective evidence is absolutely astonishing and unassailable.

I will not attempt to recite even a small part of the voluminous works of these scholars. Instead, I will merely summarize in simple terms a few of their points and the major reasons why I believe the Bible is totally trustworthy. For further research, I highly recommend the expanded book *The New Evidence That Demands a Verdict,* by my colleague Josh McDowell.

The Testimony of the Lord Jesus Christ

There is no more reliable testimony in the world than that of the Son of God—the incarnate God, the Second Person of the Godhead, the One who was the Word, who was in the beginning with God and was God, and who became flesh and dwelt among us, full of grace and truth. The record is clear that Jesus Christ believed and taught the total inerrancy of the Scriptures of His day (our Old Testament), even to the jot and tittle, the smallest characters of the Hebrew alphabet. As to the New Testament, Christ put His stamp of approval on it in advance when He said, "But the Counselor, the Holy Spirit, whom the Father will send in my name, will teach you all things and will remind you of everything that I have said to you" (John 14:26, NIV).

The Evidence of Biblical Prophecy

A most convincing evidence is that the Bible predicts future events with 100 percent accuracy, such as the fate of specific nations, including Israel. Regarding Israel and nations of the past, the predictions have come true in the most minute detail, assuring us that future events will similarly come to pass on God's schedule, including the resurrection of the dead and everlasting life. The most astonishing prophecies are the many about the birth, life, death, and resurrection of our Lord Jesus Christ, which were written hundreds of years before He was born. They came true in precise accuracy and detail, including His virgin birth, place of birth, timing of birth, details of His crucifixion, and His resurrection. At best, modern psychics, astrologers and fortune tellers have only a 50/50 chance of accuracy, whereas God's prophets are totally without error. This confirms the Scriptures as the revelation of our all-powerful God who knows and foretells the future as well as the past and present.

Evidence from Archaeology

The science of archaeology is repeatedly confirming the total accuracy of the Scriptures. In former years, before the great advance in archaeology, skeptics would claim that certain people and places were only mythical and never really existed. But doubts have been put away one by one by researchers digging and combing the ancient sites. About 200 years ago, a group of scholars listed 82 alleged "errors" in the Bible. Since then, archaeology and the increased understanding of ancient languages and cultural contexts have resolved each of them. God's Word is true in every single detail.

Evidence from the Bible's Internal Witness

Unlike any other book, the Bible consistently declares itself to be the Word of God. God even speaks in the first person! Expressions such as "And God said..." followed by God's actual words are found approximately 3,800 times, someone has counted. The apostle Paul writes, "All scripture is given by inspiration of God, and is profitable for doctrine, for reproof, for correction, for instruction in righteousness" (2 Timothy 3:16, KJV). The New International Version beautifully translates it this way: "All Scripture is God-breathed. . . ."

Evidence from the Bible's Uniqueness

There has never been another book like the Bible. It was written over a period of about 1,500 years; it was written on three continents, in three languages, Hebrew, Greek, and Aramaic; its authors were from all walks of life, from kings to peasants; and it includes hundreds of subjects. Yet the Bible has an amazing unity, consistency and continuity, making it logically beyond human ability to accomplish. It was clearly provided by an external, supernatural Guiding Hand. It was provided by God Himself.

Evidence from the Bible's Survivability

The Bible has withstood attacks not given to any other book— attacks from despots, fascists, communists, humanists, and other doubters and skeptics. Despots hate the freedom it gives to the human spirit and the worship it reserves for God alone, instead of the government. Many hate the Bible's moral imperatives. Many hate the humility it requires before Almighty God. In spite of this unparalleled opposition, the Bible has survived every attempt to destroy it. Even secular scholars admit that there are many more Bible manuscripts available—with earlier dates—than any other ancient document in existence. God has miraculously preserved His holy Word!

Evidence from the Bible's Power

The words and message of the Bible have had life-changing effects on millions of people in hundreds of languages and cultures. Through His Word, God radically changed my own life in 1944. Since then, in over 220 countries where we work, I have seen God change tens of millions of lives as His message of love and forgiveness in Jesus Christ, His only begotten Son, is shared around the world. As His Word is received and acted upon in faith, it provides the only source in the world of God's pardon, peace, purpose, and power. It tells us who we are, where we came from, where we are going, and how to get there. No other book can do that. The Bible is the inspired, inerrant Holy Word of the living God. I love it because it tells me about its Author, my wonderful Lord and Savior Jesus

Christ, as well as God the Father and God the Holy Spirit—one God manifest in three Persons. In it, God speaks to my heart and reveals His love; through it, He imparts faith; and by it, He gives me hope. To Him be all the glory and honor.

Dr. Woodrow Kroll

President and Senior Bible Teacher on the Back to the Bible Broadcast

An International Communicator Looks at the Bible

I have made it my delightful habit to read all the way through the Bible each year. So that I remember what I have read, I mark those verses that are particularly meaningful to me. That means that each year I read through another copy of the Bible.

Over these years I have made a startling discovery. If you lay out a dozen or so of my marked Bibles, often passages that I underlined one year were left without a mark a year later. Something would jump off the page at me on one occasion and lie there like a rock on another. How can this be explained? I have read other books, some of them numerous times, but this never happens when I read them. Why is that?

I have come to believe the only explanation for this is that the Bible is not just another book. It is *God's book*. It's not just a grouping of dead words, it's the revelation of the Living God. The Bible is *alive* (Hebrews 4:12). God's Word both *is* life (Philippians 2:16) and *gives* life (John 5:39). It's not easy to explain this, but it's impossible to deny it.

There are so many reasons for believing the Bible is the Word of God. It proves itself historically accurate when other ancient writings often do not. The Bible exhibits an amazing exactness with regard to prophetic events now fulfilled. The Scriptures themselves claim to be the revelation of the mind of God to the minds of men (2 Timothy 3:16). The archaeologist's trowel frequently produces discoveries that bear directly on the Bible.

But as wonderful as the Dead Sea Scrolls are, why settle for dry bones when you can have living ones. The Bible says that "if anyone is in Christ, he is a new creation; old things are passed away; behold, all things have become new" (2 Corinthians 5:17, NKJV).

I believe the most personal evidence that the Bible is God's Word is what it has done in the lives of those who have read it and believed its message. Changed lives provide the best proof that this living Book is God's Word. The most powerful evidence is the evidence of personal testimony. If the Bible is what it claims to be, then we should see lives changed by believing it. We are not disappointed.

The Changed Life of a Rabbi

There are lots of examples of the changed life recorded in the Bible, but none as dramatic as the rabbi. Saul of Tarsus sat at the feet of the great Gamaliel. He could "out-Pharisee" any of the Pharisees. The book of Acts describes his lifestyle before the message of the Bible became real to him.

We know that Saul hated the first century Christians. Obviously, as a devout Pharisee, he saw this new Christian religion as a perversion of Judaism and Jesus as nothing more than a fraud, a pseudo-messiah. At least that's the way he saw things at first. Acts 9:1–2 (NKJV) says:

Then Saul, still breathing threats and murder against the disciples of the Lord, went to the high priest and asked letters from him to the synagogues of Damascus, so that if he found any who were of the Way, whether men or women, he might bring them bound to Jerusalem.

Saul of Tarsus may well have been Christianity's greatest enemy in the first century. And then it happened. On his way to Damascus he encountered the Lord Jesus Christ and was miraculously born again. There was an immediate, noticeable, permanent change, described in Acts 9:20–21:

Immediately he preached the Christ in the synagogue, that He is the Son of God. Then all who heard were amazed, and said, "Is this not he who destroyed those who called on this name in Jerusalem, and has come here for that purpose, so that he might bring them bound to the chief priests?"

The changed life. So noticeable was the change in Saul's life that the Jews of Damascus couldn't believe it. When the message of the Bible is believed, the change in a life is dramatic. Old friends become enemies; old enemies become friends.

The Jews plotted to kill him. But their plot became known to Saul. And they watched the gates day and night, to kill him. Then the disciples took him by night and let him down through the wall in a large basket (vv. 23–25).

Saul the rabbi had studied the Old Testament scriptures with a vengeance. He hated all that Jesus of Nazareth stood for. But Saul's knowledge of the Scripture was academic, synthetic. When he met the Master, the promise of God's love conquered the rabbi's heart. Saul of Tarsus became the apostle Paul. Once the champion of Jewish persecution, now Paul was the champion of God's grace. The rabbi's life was changed forever when he understood the Bible.

The Changed Life of a Scholar

For the greater part of his life, Sir William Ramsay was a professor of humanities at the University of Aberdeen, Scotland. He was known as one of the foremost British archaeologists. He carried out extensive archaeological research in Turkey and the lands of the Bible. One of his outstanding works is entitled *St. Paul the Traveler and the Roman Citizen.* Dr. Ramsay explored the first century after Christ and especially the life and travels of the apostle Paul.

Ramsay began his book with a chapter on the trustworthiness of the book of Acts as a history of the first century. He had a special reason for doing so. In the initial chapter, Sir William Ramsay made a revealing and delightfully refreshing admission.

I may fairly claim to have entered on this investigation without any prejudice in favor of this conclusion which I shall now attempt to justify to the reader. On the contrary, I began with a mind unfavorable to it, for the ingenuity and apparent completeness of the Tubingen theory had at the time quite convinced me. It did not lie then in my line of life to investigate the subject minutely: but more recently I found myself often brought in contact with the book of Acts as an authority for the topography, antiquities, and society of Asia Minor. It was gradually borne in upon me that in various details the narrative showed marvelous truth. *

What an unusually candid admission for a scholar. He confessed his bias against the Bible—a bias that is common, but an honesty that is not. When Dr. Ramsay undertook his investigation of Asia Minor, he did so with an eye to proving the book of Acts to be an inaccurate, shabby account of the history and geography of the first century A.D. However, when he had all the evidence in hand and was able to see the real message of the book he investigated, he became a staunch supporter of the validity of the Bible.

Sir William Ramsay's days as a scholar were not over, but his days as a skeptic were. His life was changed. The critic became a Christian. The Bible has the power to change lives, even the life of a scholar.

The Changed Life of a Scoundrel

Born in London in 1722, for the most part his early life was downhill from then on. John Newton was the son of a sea captain. The sea was to be his destiny, or so he thought. Because Newton's mother died when he was seven years old, he sailed the seas with his father. With no home life and with the rough and rugged atmosphere of the sea shaping his early years, John Newton got his fill of adventure and wickedness of every kind. He grew up wild and undisciplined; he was disobedient to law of every kind and became an infidel with no education.

Later he joined the Royal Navy, but soon he deserted and was left to die on the coast of Africa. Life was hard for Newton. For more than ten years he engaged in the African slave trade. He was despicable in every sense of the word. John Newton was the perfect candidate for the power of God's Word to change his life.

When the message of the Bible is read, understood and believed by anyone, even a slave trader, that person's life is dramatically changed. Old things pass away, all things become new. That's exactly what happened to John Newton.

At age 23, Newton was miraculously converted by the grace of

---

* William M. Ramsey, *St. Paul the Traveler and the Roman Citizen* (Grand Rapids: Baker Book House, 1949), pp. 7–8.

God. He left the sea, left his old life, left everything that he once embodied behind and settled in Liverpool, England. There he came under the influence of George Whitefield and John Wesley. There he began to read God's Word. There a new future and a new career began to unfold for John Newton. He dedicated himself to religious work and finally was ordained into the ministry. He became the pastor of the parish church in Olney, England.

If you visit the church in Olney today, you will see the tombstone of John Newton. It freely admits what he once was, and also states what he became by God's grace. When Newton reflected on the difference the Word of God made in his life, he penned these words to one of the most beloved hymns of all time: "Amazing Grace, how sweet the sound, that saved a wretch like me! I once was lost but now am found, was blind but now I see."

The scoundrel became the hymn-writer. The slave trader began to trade in salvation, all because of the power of God's Word to change a life. Is the Bible the Word of God? Ask John Newton. He knows.

The Changed Life on Death Row

She lived in rural North Carolina. When Velma Barfield was charged with first degree murder, no one could have guessed what a profound effect she would have on so many people. In 1978, Barfield was arrested for brutally murdering four people. As heinous as the crime was, it looms even more reprehensible because two of those victims were her fiance and her own mother.

Velma Barfield never denied her guilt. A victim of incest as a child and the abuse of prescription drugs as an adult, Barfield was sent to prison and placed in solitary confinement. There was no hope for her; she was unredeemable, or so everyone thought.

One night a guard tuned the radio to a Christian station. The power of the radio is phenomenal. Its voice can be heard echoing down the halls of hospital wards. It can be heard humming through the marketplaces of Third World countries. Radio can climb over the walls of maximum security prisons. That night Velma Barfield heard a radio speaker teach God's Word. That night, Velma Barfield heard for the very first time that God loved her so much that He sent His Son to die for her. That night, Velma Barfield heard the message of the gospel from the Word of God. That night, Velma Barfield's life was changed forever. That night, she trusted Jesus Christ as Savior and became a new creature in Christ (2 Corinthians 5:17).

Velma Barfield's crime was real, but so was her conversion. For six years on death row she ministered to many of her cellmates. Eventually Velma wrote to Ruth Graham, wife of Evangelist Billy Graham, and there developed a real friendship. Ruth wrote to Velma: "God has turned your cell on Death Row into an unusual pulpit." Just before her final sentence, Velma wrote to Ruth: "If I am executed on August 31, I know the Lord will give me dying grace, just as He has given me saving grace, and has given me living grace."

Velma Barfield was the first woman in 22 years to be executed in the United States. She paid her debt to society, but she died knowing that Jesus Christ had paid her debt for sin. She learned that from only one book—the Bible. Velma died a free woman, free from the penalty of her sin. She died a new creature in Christ. Anyone who wants to argue that the Bible is not God's Word will have to do so with Velma Barfield. She knows differently.

The Changed Life of the "Hatchet Man"

Tough as nails. That was the personality of Charles Colson. An ex-Marine captain, *Time* magazine once described him as "tough, wily, nasty, and tenaciously loyal to Richard Nixon." Chuck Colson was proud to be President Nixon's "hatchet man."

Part of the Washington elite, a White House insider, a genuine shaker and mover, Chuck Colson was charged with doing all the "dirty work" for an administration gone wrong. But when confronted with the claims of Christ in the Word of God, Colson could resist no longer. Admitting his sin was not a problem; admitting that only Jesus could save him was. But finally, through the power of God's Word Chuck Colson was marvelously converted. He discovered the joy of a changed life.

When the news of Colson's salvation hit the newspapers it jarred Washington and the world. There was laughter from some, bewilderment from others. But the feeling of most was suspicion. How could the "hatchet man" have such a change in his life? It seemed impossible, and yet it was true. The change in Chuck Colson's life was evidence of what Paul said in 1 Corinthians, "We preach Christ crucified, to the Jews a stumbling block and to the Greeks foolishness, but to those who are called, both Jews and Greeks, Christ the power of God and the wisdom of God" (1:23–24). God's Word is God's power. It can change the life of anyone who will believe its message. That can't be said of any other book.

In Colson's own words, describing the conversation between his friend Tom Phillips and himself the night he was born again, "He (Tom) handed me his copy of *Mere Christianity.* 'Once you've read this, you might want to read the book of John in the Bible.' I scribbled notes of the key passages he quoted."* With the masterful C. S. Lewis work to appeal to his mind, and the eternal Word of God to appeal to his heart, Chuck Colson came face to face with the truth. He trusted Jesus Christ as Savior just as the Bible described, and was born again.

The White House "hatchet man" was humbled by God's grace and began immediately on a new career path—spokesman for God. There was no question in Colson's mind about whether or not the Bible is God's Word. He's an example of the changed life, changed by reading and believing the message of the Bible. The Bible is alive and can bring about a change. But only the Bible is the living Word of God.

The Changed Life of the Preacher's Kid

It was a cold March night in a little country church. A week of special meetings was in progress. The preacher was a children's evangelist—a Bible teacher who taught the Word so that children could understand it and respond. Night after night the faithful evangelist taught the Word. Night after night the church was filled. You have to picture this: The church was a one-room, country church; a crowd of 100 would fill it to capacity. There was a big potbellied stove in the middle of the church. A couple of hours before each

---

* Charles W. Colson, *Born Again* (Old Tappan, N.J.: Chosen Books, 1976), p.115.

service a deacon would arrive at the church, fire up that pot-belly stove and by the time the service began the temperature in the little church would be about 60 degrees. By the end of the service, it would be 95. So hot was the stove that the first row of pews had the paint blistered off.

Toward the end of the week, after teaching from the Bible and explaining the way of salvation, the preacher said, "It doesn't matter if your father is the pastor of this church. The Bible says that you need to trust Christ for yourself. Believe what the Bible says and your life will be changed."

When the invitation hymn was sung, only one tiny boy came forward to receive Christ. It was the pastor's son. He knew that the Bible was true. He knew he couldn't get to heaven on his parent's faith. He trusted the message of God's Word and came to the front of the little church. The preacher took the little boy to that front pew, knelt by that old pot-belly stove, and when he talked about the fires of hell, that five-year-old knew exactly what he was talking about.

Not a slave trader, not a murderer, not a Washington insider, this preacher's kid knew he needed a Savior and that Jesus Christ is the one Savior this world will ever have. That night he, too, experienced the changed life. That night he, too, became a new creature in Christ. That night he, too, became convinced that the Bible is God's Word.

I believe every example of the changed life that I have cited here is true. I know the final one is; I was that little boy.

We do not believe the Bible is God's Word just because we have experienced its power. There are many excellent philosophical, historical, textual, archaeological and theological reasons for trusting the Bible. But when it comes to us personally there is no better proof than experiencing the changing power of God's Word in our own lives.

Empirical evidence abounds to prove the trustworthiness of the Bible. We trust God's Word on the basis of the evidence. But down deep in our searching hearts, there is nothing like discovering first-hand the message of the Bible. The man with an experience is never at the mercy of the man with an argument. If you question whether or not the Bible is God's Word, set aside the arguments for a moment and experience the message. Believe what you read in the only book that's alive. Only the Bible can change your life! Only the Bible is the Living Word of God.

Dr. Adrian Rogers

Senior Pastor of the Bellevue Baptist Church of Memphis, Tennessee.

An International Pastor Looks at the Bible

I believe the Bible is the Word of God for historical reasons. Only ignorance would scoff at the impact that the Bible has had on the world. It has outlived and outranked all other books put together.

I believe the Bible is the Word of God for personal reasons. The best people that I have known—the wisest, the kindest, the most sacrificial—have all given allegiance to the Bible as the inspired Word of God. Correspondingly, in my own personal life it is not how I feel but what I know coming from the pages of God's Word that enables me to maintain Christian character and constancy. My personal life, my professional life, and my home life are radically transformed by the truths of God's Word.

I believe the Bible is the Word of God for logical reasons. The more I study the Bible the more intrinsic and hidden beauty I see. It is totally, completely inconceivable that the Bible could have been written by human authorship alone. It is too intricately interwoven. It is too profoundly true. It is too prophetically accurate to be anything less than the Word of God.

I believe the Bible to be the Word of God for spiritual reasons. When I read the Bible, I hear the Holy Spirit of God bearing witness that these words are true. He is the One who wrote it through human penmen, and He is the One who illumines it so that I can understand it and confirms it to my heart.

I believe the Bible is the Word of God for theological reasons. The Bible testifies of Jesus—the Living Word—and the Living Word—Jesus—testifies of the Bible, the Written Word. In my opinion, they rise and fall together.

Alfred Edersheim

A Timeless Historian Looks at the Bible

The celebrated scholar Alfred Edersheim published *The Bible History, Old Testament* in 1876–77. In this massive work Edersheim states his conviction that the Bible is truly God's Word and the confirmation of our faith is reasonable, saying:

"For the Bible should be viewed, not only in its single books, but in their connection, and in the unity of the whole. The Old Testament could not be broken off from the New, and each considered as independent of the other. Nor yet could any part of the Old Testament be disjoined from the rest. The full meaning and beauty of each appears only in the harmony and unity of the whole. Thus they all form lines of one unbroken chain, reaching from the beginning to the time when the Lord Jesus came for who all the previous history had prepared, to whom all the types pointed, and in whom all the promises are 'Yea and Amen.' Then that which God had spoken to Abraham, more than two thousand years before, became a blessed reality, 'for the Scripture, foreseeing that God would justify the heathen through faith, preached before the gospel to Abraham, saying, In thee shall all nations be blessed. So then they which be of faith are blessed with faithful Abraham.' That this one grand purpose should have been steadily kept in view, and carried forward through all the vicissitudes of history, changes of time, and stages of civilization—and that without any apparent alteration, only further unfolding and at last completion—affords indeed the strongest affirmation of our faith. . . .

"There is not merely harmony but also a close connection between the various parts of Scripture. Each book illustrates the other, taking up its teaching and carrying it forward. Thus the unity of Scripture is not like that of a stately building, however ingenious its plan or vast its proportions; but rather, to use a Biblical illustration, like that of the light, which shineth more and more to the perfect day. We mark throughout growth in its progress, as men were able to bear fuller communications, and prepared for their reception. The Law, the types, the history, the prophecies, and the promises of the Old Testament all progressively unfold and develop the same truth, until it appears at last in its New Testament fullness. Though all testify to the same thing, not one of them can be easily left out, nor yet do we fully understand any one part unless we view it in its bearing and connection with the others. And so when at last we come to the close of Scripture, we see how the account of the creation and of the first calling of the children of God, which had been recorded in the book of Genesis, has found it full counterpart—its *fulfillment*—in the book of Revelation, which tells the glories of the second creation, and the perfecting of the Church of God. As one of the old Church teachers (St. Augustine) writes:

> *'Novum Testamentum in vetere latet,*
> *Vetus in novo patet.'* *

"That in a work composed of so many books, written under such very different circumstances, by penmen so different, and at periods so widely apart there should be 'some things hard to be understood, which they that are unlearned and unstable wrest,' can surely not surprise us, more particularly when we remember that it was God's purpose only to send the brighter light as men were able to bear it. Besides, we must expect that with our limited powers and knowledge we shall not be able fully to understand the ways of God. But, on the other hand this may be safely said, that the more deep, calm, and careful our study, the more ample the evidence it will bring to light to confirm our faith against all the attacks of the enemy."

---

* *Translation:* 'The New Testament is latent in the Old;
            the Old is patent (evident) in the New.'

Josh McDowell

An International Apologist Looks at the Bible

Most of us have heard of the "wonders of the ancient world" including the pyramids of Egypt, the hanging gardens of Babylon, the Colossus of Rhodes, and so on. Let's look at eight of these "wonders of the Bible" that contribute to its uniqueness as God's Holy Word.

The Wonder of Its Unity

One of the most amazing characteristics of the Bible is unity, which is evident in spite of its being a compilation of 66 books written over a period of 1500 years. The books of the Bible were composed by more than 40 authors from a variety of educational and cultural backgrounds. Joshua, for example, was a military general; Daniel the prophet was a prime minister; Amos was a shepherd; Peter and John, fishermen; and Nehemiah a court servant. The 66 books were composed in a variety of places and cultures. Ezekiel wrote his work while a captive in Babylon. The apostle Paul wrote some of his letters from prison in Rome. David the king wrote some of his psalms while he was a fugitive in the wilderness. Jeremiah wrote while he was in a dungeon. The books were written on three continents: Africa, Asia, and Europe. The Bible was composed in three languages. The Old Testament was written mostly in Hebrew, with a small part in Aramaic. The New Testament was composed in the common Greek of the day, *Koine*. The Bible deals with a variety of controversial subjects such as the origin of the universe, the existence and nature of God, the nature and purpose of mankind, and the origin and extent of evil. One would expect that the result of all this diversity would be a hodgepodge of contradictory literature—a chaotic text, full of contradictions and distortions. We see the wonder of the Bible in that it is completely consistent, coherent, and trustworthy—forming one cohesive whole, one dynamic message of God's dealing with mankind.

The unity of the Bible is consistent from beginning to end. These teachings include the following:

Man—his origin, his fall, his redemption, his earthly and eternal destiny.

Sin—its beginning, its consequences, its punishment in this world and the next.

Satan—the instigator of evil, the liar and murderer from the beginning, his war against God and against believers, his final judgment.

Israel—her social and political development, idolatry, preservation and final destiny.

The Church—her history, from her establishment to her glorification.

Salvation—its provision, according to the divine plan.

Repentance, faith, the life of the believer, prayer, the service of God, etc.—subjects for infinitely rewarding study, carrying us through the entire Bible.

The Holy Spirit—present at creation, pronouncing the last prayer of the Bible (Genesis 1:2, Revelation 22:17).

God—forever the same, in His sovereignty, His eternality, His spirituality, his omnipotence, His uniqueness, His omniscience, His omnipresence, His holiness, His righteousness, and His love.

Jesus Christ—the theme *par excellence* of all written revelation.*

The Wonder of Its Accuracy

Another feature that separates the Bible from other ancient literature is its meticulous fidelity to historical and scientific accuracy. Within the pages of the Bible, we find continuous references to events, people, and places. The science of archaeology along with secular historical records confirms the precision of the references in the various Biblical books. The minute attention to

* Rene Pache, *Inspiration and Authority* (Chicago: Moody Press, 1970), pp. 116–117.

detail observed by the Biblical writers is unparalleled in any other ancient literature. Nelson Glueck, a famous Jewish archaeologist, observed, "It may be stated categorically that no archaeological discovery has ever controverted a Biblical reference. . . . [I assert] the almost incredibly accurate historical memory of the Bible, and particularly so when it is fortified by archaeological fact."

The Bible is not a scientific textbook and is not written in scientific language. It is primarily a record of God's dealings with humankind as well as a promise of God's future blessings in the eternal kingdom for those who love Him. Yet, whenever its writers touch on scientific matters in their narratives, their observations about nature, man, history, and society are accurate. Their observations are also remarkably free of the ancient and unsophisticated scientific inaccuracies of their contemporaries. For example, there are vast differences between the historically sound accounts of creation found in the Bible and the absurd, mythological accounts of creation popular at the same time in other cultures.

The Wonder of Its Indestructibility

The fact that the complete text of the Bible has survived throughout history is a wonderful testimony to the preserving power of God. The Scripture has survived time, persecution, and criticism.

The first book of the Bible was composed some 3500 years ago; the last was completed nearly 2000 years ago. The original manuscripts were all written on perishable surfaces and have long since disappeared. The thousands of copies we possess, however, accurately represent the originals. Through the science of textual criticism, from these copies we can arrive at a very close reproduction of the originals. The overwhelming manuscript evidence of the text of the Old and New Testaments affirms that the text of the Bible has not only survived throughout the centuries, but has survived virtually unchanged.

The Bible has also survived despite the persecution of believers over the centuries. In A.D. 303 the Roman emperor Diocletian wrote an imperial letter ordering (1) the destruction of all Christian churches, (2) the burning of all Christian Scriptures, and (3) the loss of civil liberties by all professing Christians. That did not stop the spread of Christianity or the proclamation of God's revelation in the Bible. Constantine, the Roman emperor who succeeded Diocletian, converted to Christianity and eventually ordered 50 copies of the Scriptures to be produced by the best scribes at government expense.

The Scriptures have also survived criticism. No other book has been subjected to such thorough criticism as has been leveled at the Bible. Yet the Bible is equal to that challenge, and has withstood the most rigorous criticism imaginable.

The testimony is clear. Time passes, but the Bible remains a dramatic testimony to the keeping power of God for His revelation. Rulers come and go. The Bible remains. Critics come and go. The Bible remains. The prophet Isaiah, speaking 2700 years ago, declared, "All flesh is grass, and all its loveliness is like the flower of the field. The grass withers, the flower fades, when the breath of the Lord blows upon it; surely the people are grass. The grass withers, the flower fades, but the word of the Lord stands forever" (Isaiah 40:6–8, NASB).

The Wonder of Its Frankness

An amazing feature of the Bible is the frankness with which it deals with frailties of the people of God and even the shortcomings of its own authors. The Bible paints a realistic portrait of its characters, resisting the temptation to mythologize or perfect them. For example, the Bible does not conceal the failures and poor choices of great men of God such as Noah, Abraham, King David, and the apostles. The fact that the personalities in the Bible are flawed does not detract from the Biblical message: it is the holiness of the Lord God that the Bible proclaims, not the perfection of His followers and prophets. Yet the greatest personality revealed in the Bible, the one of whom in some sense the whole Bible speaks, is described as being without sin, as perfect and holy as His Father. The perfect one is Jesus Christ our Lord.

The Wonder of Its Predictive Prophecy

One of the most incredible features of the Bible is its predictive prophecy. In no other books do we find the wealth of prophecies, clearly made years before their fulfillment. And all accurately fulfilled in history. Predictive prophesy was given to inform mankind of the nature and attributes of the Lord God and of His goals for His creation.

The most important prophecies, some fulfilled and some yet to be fulfilled, concern Jesus Christ. The Old Testament contains dozens of prophecies about the coming Savior and deliverer of God's people, the Messiah of Israel. Christ's work of salvation for mankind through His sacrifice on the cross fulfilled many of them. Some still wait for their fulfillment at the Second Coming, when the Lord returns from heaven in judgment and victory.

The Wonder of Its Christ-Centeredness

Another unique and wonderful feature of the Bible is Christ-centeredness. The Bible, from beginning to end, in both Old and New Testaments, is a testimony to Jesus Christ, the "Son of Man" and the Lord of Glory. After the resurrection, Christ Himself explains how the Scriptures center on Him:

"'O foolish men and slow of heart to believe in all that the prophets have spoken! Was it not necessary for the Christ to suffer these things and to enter into His glory?' Then beginning with Moses and all the prophets, He explained to them the things concerning Himself in all the Scriptures" (Luke 24:25–27, NASB).

The Old Testament records the preparation for the coming of the Messiah. The Gospels record the coming of the Messiah, Jesus Christ our Lord. The book of Acts records the propagation of the gospel (the good news) concerning Jesus Christ. The epistles (letters) explain the gospel and its implications for our lives. The book of Revelation anticipates and describes the Second Coming of Jesus Christ and the establishment of His eternal kingdom. From beginning to end, the Bible glorifies Jesus Christ and centers on Him.

The Wonders of Its Teachings

Another wonderful aspect of the Bible separates it from all other religious books and is a testimony to its divine origin. This is the wonder of its unique teachings. The teachings in the Bible cannot be explained as a product of the religious environment of its authors, since many of its teachings were contrary to contemporary religious thought and were hard for the Jews themselves to accept. For example, much of the unique teaching in the Bible centers around the personal God it reveals. Israel was surrounded by polytheistic cultures (cultures that believed in more than one God). Israel often slipped into idolatry itself. Yet its holy Scriptures—the Old Testament—betray not a word in favor of idolatry or polytheism. The Old Testament, in fact, is replete with warnings against idolatry and with condemnation of idolaters. In addition, the Bible repeatedly emphasizes the monotheism (belief in one God) which is the bulwark of Biblical theology.

The nature and attributes of the God of the Bible are also different from the concepts of God in cultures surrounding the Jews. The Bible reveals a God who is infinite and personal, who cares for human beings as a Father and who personifies love, respect, justice, and mercy. This is in contrast to other gods of the ancient world who were to be obeyed and served out of fear rather than from loving respect.

In many other religious settings, God is to be obeyed in order for the faithful to receive rewards. In the Bible we are taught to obey God out of love: "If you love Me, you will keep My commandments" (John 14:15, NASB).

A final unique teaching from the Bible is the resurrection of the founder of Christianity, Jesus Christ. This teaching is a wonder, since in no other religious literature do we have a resurrection that was *bodily* and that can be *tested* by the most rigorous historical methods. While many other religious traditions have ideas of spiritual or spirit resurrections (untestable hypotheses), only the Bible proclaims a bodily resurrection that passes all tests of historical reliability.

The Wonder of Its Life-Transforming Power

This wonder personalizes the facts and evidences about which we have been talking, addressing itself to the individual. This wonder is the Bible's effect on individuals. If the Bible is indeed the Word of God, it should demonstrate its ability to transform lives in harmony with its message of eternal life. We must first note that the Bible claims that it can transform lives, filling the spiritual void within all people.

Let's look at the words of Christ:

Matthew 11:28–30, NASB

"Come to Me, all who are weary and heavy-laden, and I will give you rest. Take My yoke upon you and learn from Me, for I am gentle and humble in heart, and you will find rest for your souls. For My yoke is easy and My burden is light."

John 4:14, NASB

"Whoever drinks of the water that I will give him shall never thirst; but the water that I will give him shall become in him a well of water springing up to eternal life."

Matthew 5:6, NASB

"Blessed are those who hunger and thirst for righteousness, for they shall be satisfied."

John 5:39, NASB

"You search the Scriptures because you think that in them you have eternal life; and it is these that testify about Me."

E. Y. Mullins gives this perspective on the life-transforming importance of the Scriptures:

"I have, for me at least, irrefutable evidence of the objective existence of the Person so moving me. When to this personal experience I add that of tens of thousands of living Christians, and an unbroken line of them back to Christ, and when I find in the New Testament a manifold record of like experiences, together with a clear account of the origin and cause of them all, my certainty becomes absolute. One of the most urgent of all duties resting upon modern Christians is to assert with clearness and vigor the certainties of Christian experience."

For millions of people, this life-transforming power is evident as they read God's revelation in the Bible and encounter the person of Jesus Christ the Savior. The wonderful, life-transforming power of the Bible is a fact. For 2000 years it has been transforming lives like no other literary work, and it is still doing it today. It has certainly changed my life, and I pray it has changed yours.

These evidences, and others, make it clear that the Bible is not just another book, but a wonderful record of God's voice to humankind. It is truly the Word of God.

Colonel Dan Davis, D. Min.

A Military Veteran Looks at the Bible

The expectations of ministry placed upon military chaplains demands the very best of them in belief and in behavior. They live and minister within the context of a pluralistic society that primarily exists for fighting the nation's wars. To this community of many faiths, and some of no faith at all, they are expected to bring God to men and men to God. And in doing so, even though they are separated from the traditional lines of like-clergy support enjoyed by civilian clergy, they must nevertheless faithfully represent the church or denomination which endorses them to the military chaplaincy ministry.

Most religious groups recognized for endorsing men and women to the military chaplaincy go to great lengths to determine that the candidate is properly prepared on at least four fronts: theological, philosophical, mental and physical. Of the four, as far as the endorsing church or denomination is concerned, the area of paramount importance is that of the theological. It is important to the endorser that the chaplain candidate be well grounded in theological beliefs and concepts. It is also important to be assured that the chaplain candidate will stand faithful in his/her calling in the midst of demanding ministry and of colleagues who hold different views.

It is always anticipated that military chaplains will be expected to work on the cutting edge of ministry. Often their ministry is performed in circumstances and situations that can only be classified as extreme. Of all the involvements in life, there are few experiences that are more extreme than that of battle. In such extremes the military chaplain is expected always to behave in a way that will bring credit to his/her God, the nation, the unit to which assigned, and to him/herself. The chaplain is expected to rise above fear and to do his/her duty, that of bringing to hurting people the message of comfort and hope provided by the Living God, usually through His Holy Word, the Bible. Men and women caught up in one of humanity's most tragic activities deserve a sure word from divinely inspired Scripture by which they will be able to find the encouragement to face life, and sometimes death. They need to hear that sure word from one who believes it him/herself, and who communicates it with a sense of quiet confidence.

Several years ago the constitutionality of the U. S. Military Chaplaincy was tested through a lawsuit that essentially said that maintaining this religious activity was a violation of the principle calling for the separation of Church and State. Those who made the complaint felt that a civilian clergy could provide adequate religious coverage to military personnel on a day-by-day basis. The Supreme Court settled the matter by deciding in favor of the long-established chaplaincy program. Their basic rationale for doing so was simply that every member of the military had the right of the free exercise of religion, both in peace and in war. The civilian clergy, lacking the training needed for a battlefield ministry, could not effectively accompany the military into battle, and thus could not ensure the right of free exercise.

Ministry in the name of God is a cherished priority for all chaplains. Battlefield ministry in the name of God is a high privilege. There are many things that have already been written in pamphlets, military manuals, and other books about how chaplains are to conduct ministry in times of war. But when it is all "sifted" and brought down to basics, battlefield ministry is characterized by simplicity. The trappings of tradition and denominational expression are set aside for a more direct involvement. For example: taking time for a brief worship service while preparing for battle, holding a quick prayer service with a group of soldiers who are only minutes away from departure to engage the enemy, sitting in a foxhole with a soldier and reading the Word of God and praying together for strength and protection, kneeling by a wounded soldier in an aid tent and audibly praying the Lord's Prayer. All of these ministries must be in their simplest form—that of proclaiming a caring God and the truths of His Holy Word.

There are few times in providing ministry in a pre-battle, battle, or post-battle situation that the chaplain does not turn to sacred Scripture. In it are words of life, of comfort, encouragement and hope. The chaplain communicates these truths to those to whom ministry is being provided in many ways, not the least of which is the quiet assurance expressed in attitude and expression that what is being shared from God's Word is sincerely believed.

Asked to write this article on why I believe that the Bible is true from the perspective of a military chaplain, it seemed to me that it should be written with a major emphasis upon the most unique aspect of doing business for God within a military setting—that of the battlefield ministry. In the midst of the turmoil associated with battlefield ministry there is precious little time, if any, for refining theological concepts, or for apologetics. There is time only for stepping forth with a heart in tune with God and His all-encompassing Word.

It is my opinion that what a chaplain believes with reference to whether the Bible is true or not will definitely affect his/her battlefield ministry. It will make a significant difference in the quality and success of the ministry provided. When soldiers face the fear of the unknown, they are not well cared for by an individual who doubts the source of his/her spiritual words. Little encouragement is received by those in spiritual need when the spiritual provider has difficulty in believing his/her own message. What a chaplain believes about God, about His Word, and the application of that Word in times of ministry in the extreme, makes a difference.

There is no doubt in my mind that the Bible is the Word of God and that it is true from Genesis to Revelation. As a Christian, the God of truth is the Foundation of my being (Acts 17:28). As a servant of this loving God of truth, and more specifically as one called of God to be a military chaplain, I have learned to depend upon His truth, the highest expression of which is the Bible.

In the following comments on why I believe that the Bible is true, I have intentionally set aside any discussion of the traditional technical reasons for my belief in the truth of the Word of God for a more practical approach. I have chosen to write about my experiences of ministry as a military chaplain who has long trusted the Word of God and depended upon its truths. What I have believed about the Word of God has been validated time and again through my ministry experience. As the truth of the Bible has worked its way into the warp and woof of my life, its expressions through my service to the Lord Jesus Christ have resulted in blessings to others and a steadfast personal hope that daily sustains my living (Romans 5:4). The Bible tells me that I can expect God's involvement in my life. My experience tells me it is so. I believe that the Bible is true because I have experienced God's protection, His presence and His promise.

God's evident protection in my life began early in my active-duty ministry as an army chaplain. In May 1970, I was serving as a reserve component chaplain in the Alabama National Guard, namely as the Assistant Group Chaplain of the 20th Special Forces Group, a National Guard Green Beret unit. At that time my denomination invited me to leave the National Guard for active duty with the U.S. Army, and more specifically, with duty as a Green Beret Chaplain with the troops in Vietnam. In those days the struggles of the Vietnam war seemed to encompass the world. In Vietnam suffering was everywhere. The young military men and women were caught up in a hated war that brought to them both mental and physical wounds, and often death. Others were somehow, in the chaos and confusion of battle, lost and unaccounted for. Still others were captured and subjected to the inhumane treatment often visited upon prisoners of war (POWs). Everyone despised the necessity of involvement in a frightful conflict in which they seldom even saw the enemy. "Do the job called for." "Survive." "Go back home." These were the paramount thoughts of people in the uniforms of their country facing the uncertainties of being involved in one of man's most tragic endeavors. They sought for help where they could find it. Chaplains, with their commitment to battlefield ministry, were always welcome.

Here in the United States many struggled to understand the war. Some were strongly opposed for whatever reason. They made their views known by demonstrating against the war. They marched in the streets, burned their draft cards, refused to report for military duty, left the country, wrote and published their objections, and visited the enemy. Families whose sons and daughters answered the call of their country to serve learned of the welfare of their young military people through various types of correspondence, newspaper and television reports. The news received was often good; at other times it was tragic. Their loved one had been wounded and hurt, was missing in action, had been listed as a POW, or had died serving the country.

The clergy of every denomination were extremely busy in those days. They rejoiced with the various families whose sons and daughters came home and they suffered with the families that received the bodies of cherished progeny lost to an early death. They brought words of hope and encouragement to families whose loved ones were missing in action or had been declared POWs. To the clergy was relegated the responsibilities of helping their people to cope with the vicissitudes of an unpopular war, and to make sense of death and dying in such a war.

Of such was my ministry during the decade of the '60s. Then came the invitation to serve as an Army chaplain on active duty. I accepted the call of my church to provide ministry to the military with the understanding that I would almost immediately be assigned to Vietnam with duty as a Special Forces chaplain. This meant that I would be in many places throughout Vietnam as I sought to provide ministry. It would necessitate the accompaniment of troops into battle, traveling alone to areas where my troops anticipated battle, eating and sleeping where I could.

I thought at length about this. I knew something of the Vietnam war and its enormous difficulties. The possibility of being wounded or dying came to mind. I felt that, in faith, I was ready to deal with these. But the possibility of being captured and suffering months and years as a POW subject to the whims of the enemy was something that I found extremely difficult to accept. Often I would lie awake at night thinking of it, dreading the thought of it, and fearing the prospect. I knew that I would need God's protection.

I brought the situation to God in prayer and Bible study. Day after day, as I awaited the day to report to active duty, I sought

God's face with a sense of hope for a specific answer to my need for the assurance of His protection. Then one day as I prayerfully read from the Scriptures, God answered! He spoke to my heart through His Word!

Proverbs 3:21–26

> My son, let not them depart from thine eyes: keep sound wisdom and discretion: so shall they be life unto thy soul and grace to thy neck. Then shalt thou walk in thy way safely, and thy foot shall not stumble. When thou liest down, thou shalt not be afraid: yea, thou shalt lie down, and thy sleep shall be sweet. Be not afraid of sudden fear, neither of the desolation of the wicked, when it cometh. For the Lord shall be thy confidence, and shall keep thy foot from being taken.

My spirit leaped within me. It was God's personal answer to my prayer for protection. I wrote in my Bible: "Praise Jesus! My blessed and sweet Protection!" Fear and anxiety over the possibility of being taken captive by the enemy faded.

It was replaced with a quiet confidence that God would be my Protector. This confidence has not failed. Time and time again across the years God has spoken to my heart through the Bible with the assurance of His protection. Always He has been faithful and true. Never have I been disappointed. In years of ministry as a paratrooper, in months of ministry in hostile areas, and in military operations in various parts of the world, always, I have made my way in the service of Christ constantly aware of the divine protection promised me in the Bible. Again I declare for all to hear and understand: I believe that the Bible is true because I have experienced God's unceasing protection as revealed to me in the Holy Scriptures.

I also believe that the Bible is true because I have experienced God's faithful presence in my life. In the military system no one goes unidentified. The uniform worn bears various symbols which indicate the individual's name, unit, job expertise, and rank. The chaplain is easily recognized. On occasion, when the chaplain approaches a group of troops someone in the group will say, "Here comes the Chaplain. Watch your language." Early in my chaplaincy ministry I wondered what that kind of recognition really meant. Was it respect for the chaplain as a person, or was it respect for

God? I learned that it is a bit of the former and a great deal of the latter. No doubt there is respect for the chaplain as a person since the chaplain is certainly a legitimate part of the military family. However, after almost four decades of military service from the rank of private to full colonel, I am convinced that the greater reason for the deference shown is that the troops sense the presence of the transcendent God when one known as "the Chaplain" comes into their midst. It's a truth that humbles the heart and makes glad the spirit.

When Jesus charged His disciples with taking the good news of the gospel into all the world, He said: "And, lo, I am with you alway, even unto the end of the world" (Matthew 28:20:b). This was a declaration on the part of Jesus that is not up for debate. It is a truth of God's Word that has been experienced by multiplied millions of the Christian faith. What joy there is to daily walk in the presence of the Triune God. As the Bible stated that it would be, the presence of Christ is with his own.

Having experienced this truth revealed in the Word of God, the leaders in the military chaplaincy talk much about the ministry of Presence. The idea behind the ministry of Presence is simply that which has already been stated—military people sense the transcendent presence of God when the chaplain is on the scene. This is a Presence in the world of battle that soldiers and leaders alike desire. It brings the blessings and hope of Him who gives life and who takes it away.

Personally I have experienced God's presence in more occasions of ministry than memory recalls. There is one incident, however, that stands out. It was an occasion when the Biblical truth that Christ would be present was fully tested.

It was early in the day at Nha Trang when I learned that one of our Special Forces units based in Kontom was expecting an attack from the Viet Cong that night. Knowing the power of the ministry of Presence, I caught a "chopper" and made my way to the Kontom-based unit. When I arrived at the camp, the soldiers were busy constructing a berm around the campsite. On top of the berm they placed their heavy 50-caliber machine guns, while others dug in behind the berm—for protection when they used their personal weapons.

The men took their places as night fell. We waited for the attack that our intelligence had predicted. During the wait it was my privilege to go from soldier to soldier. Moving low and as quietly as possible, I would crawl into their dugout positions. As I spoke with each man, it did not take long for the conversation to turn to God and the comfort of His Word.

The final point that I came to that night was a machine gun position. It was manned by a seasoned soldier whom I had known in an earlier assignment. "How's it going, Top?"* "Not so good, Chaplain. I am glad you are here. Not sure we will make it through the night. We need all the help we can get." "Are you afraid?" "Sure." "Top, I have learned from the Bible that the love of God casts out all fear, and that love can be ours when we give our hearts to Jesus Christ, making Him our Savior and Lord. Are you interested?" "Well, I have certainly thought about it many times, Chaplain. Yeah, I guess I am interested." "Then why don't we pray together." And pray we did.

There was no doubt in my mind that the presence of the Holy Spirit was there and that He was doing a work of grace and mercy in this soldier's life. That Green Beret, a seasoned veteran of many years of military service, experienced the presence of God in his life that night in a way that he had never known before. "How is it now, Top?" "It's a whole lot better, Chaplain. I sure do thank you." We prayed again to thank God for His faithfulness and for Top's deliverance from the bondage of fear and sin. And then I left his side to attend to other opportunities to express the truth of the Bible, that the presence of Christ would be with us.

Some say that battlefield conversions do not last. Well, I cannot speak for all of them, but for the one recounted above I have a further word. Ten years later at Ft. Bragg, North Carolina, I was preaching in the John F. Kennedy Chapel in the Special Forces area. When I walked to the pulpit, I looked out over the congregation. There, sitting to my left, toward the back of the chapel, was Top. He, his

---

* "Top": First Sergeant (top-ranking N.C.O.).

wife and his three children lined the pew. I could not help but ask, "How's it going, Top?" His response: "It has never been the same, Chaplain. I have been walking with the Lord since that night on the berm in Kontom." God had made the Bible as true for him as He had for me.

You ask me why I believe that the Bible is true. I believe it is true for a myriad of reasons, but essentially because I have experienced its truth in the protection of God and in the assurance of His abiding presence. Further, I have experienced that the Bible is true through the kept promises of God.

"God is not a man, that he should lie; neither the son of man, that he should repent: hath he said, and shall he not do it? or hath he spoken, and shall he not make it good?" (Numbers 23:19). What God promises in His Word, He fulfills. What God promises in the midst of any situation will surely come to pass.

In 1991 it was my privilege to be the senior chaplain for VII Corps during Operation Desert Shield/Desert Storm. We had assembled in the deserts of Saudi Arabia the largest heavy Corps in the history of the U.S. Army. Our Abram tanks and Bradley fighting vehicles numbered in the thousands. There were 140,000 men and women assigned to the Corps.

We had come to the Persian Gulf area to convince Saddam Hussein of Iraq that he must withdraw his forces from Kuwait, a small oil-rich country seated on the waters of the Persian Gulf. We had hoped to do so with a "show of force" on the part of a coalition of forces from several nations. Daily we prayed that Saddam would peaceably relinquish his ill-gotten gain and would pull his troops and equipment back to his own country. The President of the United States drew a line in the sand. He gave Saddam until midnight on January 16, 1991, to withdraw. If he did not do so we would begin bombing his forces. Saddam paid the President no attention. True to his word, the order went out for the bombing to commence. At 2:45 a.m. on January 17 the bombing of Iraq's military positions began. Of course, many of us were disappointed that our prayer for a peaceful solution to the problem was not found.

An important command and control unit of the VII Corps during battle was its Tactical Operations Center (TAC). It was the nerve center of the Corps' immediate deployment of its tactical might on the battlefield. From this center, far forward in the area of conflict, the Commanding General directed his portion of the coalition forces. His mission was to employ the VII Corps as the spearpoint of the thrust against the armor-heavy Iraqi army, the fourth largest army in the world.

On January 14, three days before the bombings began, I held a worship service for the members of the VII Corps (TAC). We fervently prayed that somehow God would deliver us from the need of battle, that we would not have to drop the first bomb or fire a shot in anger, that Saddam Hussein would come to his senses and capitulate. After the service we went away with a quiet hope in our heart that God would grant our requests.

When the bombing started on January 17 we knew that the desire of our hearts for deliverance from battle was not to be. On January 18 I was called by the Corps TAC to return to their area for another worship service. Just before the worship service, knowing that I needed to give those in attendance some explanation as to why God had not answered our prayer desires, I walked out into the desert to be alone with God. I told Him that I was disappointed that we were now going to be forced into battle with the Iraqi military might with its half million men, thousands of tanks, armored vehicles and other weapons of war. I asked God for a word from Him that I could pass on to our soldiers.

And God spoke to my heart!

He said that Saddam Hussein's ability to wage war had to come to an end. God said there were two reasons for this: That there could never be peace in the Middle East as long as Saddam had the military might he needed to attack his neighbors, and that Israel could never prosper as long as she had to live under Saddam's threat. God also said that the United States Military and the coalition forces were instruments of His righteousness for the destruction of Iraq's military might.

I said that I understood, but that my heart was pained with the prospects of losing thousands of our young soldiers to accomplish this God-given task. My mind went back to the days in Vietnam and the great grief experienced by families whose loved ones were lost in battle. And I thought of the hundreds of immediate family members (spouses and children) who were awaiting our return to Germany, the place of our deployment to the Persian Gulf area. If thousands of us were to die in this foreign land, there would be many more thousands of loved ones in another foreign land who would grieve their loss without support from their extended families. Their suffering would be too much.

And God said that I was not to worry . . . that we would have victory without great casualty.

After this time alone with God in the desert, I conducted the worship services called for by our soldiers at the TAC. In the service I told them exactly what God had told me. There was a quiet sense of awe and reverence among us. It was mingled with a sense of the pending blessings of God. What He had promised, we anticipated.

As the bombing continued, the plans for the ground attack upon the Iraqis was being finalized. We were to launch the attack against the elite Republican Guard Force of the Iraqi army on February 24. On the night of February 21, I visited with the 1st Armored Division. The Division Chaplain invited me to speak with his Commanding General. The CG and I talked awhile and our conversation soon turned to the upcoming attack, an attack that the 1st Armored Division would spearhead. Like any great general, he was burdened over the prospects of soldiers dying in battle. He anticipated a loss of 2,000 people. He communicated his heaviness of heart to me. With a good deal of apprehension I told him that he need not worry, that God had spoken to my heart and had promised that we would have victory without great casualty. He gave me an unusual look and said, "Do you really think so?" My response was simply that it was a promise that God had given to me under the desert skies, and that God could not lie.

Early in the morning of February 24, the day of the ground attack, I was with the VII Corps Commanding General at the Corps main headquarters. He was giving the final briefing to his people before launching the attack. Though he anticipated the loss of 5,000 men in the battle, he was confident of success. He looked over to me and said, "Chaplain, I don't think we are going to get to church today. Will you lead us in prayer?" I prayed for God's blessings upon our forces and efforts, and for victory without great casualty.

On February 28, after 100 hours of war, the Iraqis were soundly defeated. They had lost at least 3,000 main battle tanks, hundreds of armored fighting vehicles, and thousands of soldiers whose bodies were strewn everywhere on the battlefield. The losses for the 1st Armored Division, spearhead Division for the Corps, was a total of four people. Total losses for the VII Corps that had deployed 144,000 men (including the 1st Armored Division) was 49 people. God had indeed answered prayer and was true to His word. We had victory without great casualty! The senior Commanding General of the Coalition Forces called our exceptionally small number of casualties a "miracle." And it was a miracle, one that came from God whose Word, the Bible, teaches us that we can count on His promises.

The Psalmist, David, declared: "I have been young, and now am old; yet have I not seen the righteous forsaken, nor his seed begging bread" (Psalm 37:25). I trust that I will not appear to be presumptuous by aligning myself with David. I was a tender young man when God called me to the ministry and further called me to serve Him as an army chaplain. After forty-four years of Gospel ministry (thirty of it serving as a military chaplain), I have never seen the time that my experiences did not confirm the truth as revealed in the Bible. There is no doubt in my military mind that the Bible is true. In the many life-experiences of more than six decades I have been the recipient, time and time again, of God's gracious protection, His merciful presence, and His faithful promises. They have not come as a surprise to me. I learned from the Bible what I could expect from my Living Lord. He has far exceeded my expectations. THE BIBLE REALLY IS TRUE!

Dr. Stephen F. Olford

A Renowned Homiletician Looks at the Bible

2 Timothy 3:14–17; 1 Peter 1:22–25; 2 Peter 1:19–21

Someone once said that even though heaven, earth, the visible church, and man himself, crumbled into nonentity, he would, through grace, hold on to the Word of God as the unbreakable link between his soul and God. That man believed the Bible—and so must we, in a day of human speculation and hopeless uncertainty.

Our texts teach that the Bible claims for itself: (1) infallibility, for it is the "word of the Lord" (1 Pet. 1:25); (2) indestructibility, for it "endures forever"; and (3) indispensability: it is "the word of good tidings which was preached unto [men]." Let us consider this threefold basis for belief in the Bible:

1. The Infallibility of the Bible

"The word of the Lord" (1 Pet. 1:25). By infallibility we are not implying that all the actions recorded in the Bible have divine approval, nor that the words reported have divine authority. In other words, we do not defend Jacob's deception of his father, nor David's sins of immorality and murder. Nor do we mean that the present-day translations and renderings of the original autographs are faultless, for anyone familiar with translations will admit that there have been discrepancies in the medium of expression. At the same time, it is important to note that over 1,150 Old Testament manuscripts exist in the original language that have been examined by Hebrew scholars and proved to be in agreement with each other in essential points. The number is even higher for New Testament manuscripts. With that negative backdrop we can positively state that "the word of the Lord"—the Bible—is:

A. God's Infallible Record to Men

"The word of the Lord" (1 Pet. 1:25). Note the Bible's claim for itself. It is a record which is:

1. Divinely Inspired

"All Scripture is given by inspiration of God" (2 Tim. 3:16). Inspiration has been defined as "the supernatural activity of God on the human mind by which the apostles, prophets and sacred writers were qualified to set forth divine truth without any admixture of error." The validity of this definition can be illustrated by the miracle of the Bible's unity. The Bible was written over a period of 1,500 years by nearly forty authors of different backgrounds. It was penned in three distinct languages—Hebrew, Aramaic and Greek—in countries far apart; yet the entire book is a harmonious whole. Dr. R. A. Torrey says that "the Bible is not a superficial unity, but a profound unity." Such unity in diversity can only be accounted for by the fact that the Bible has one Author—the Holy Spirit. Then there is the miracle of the Bible's accuracy. Take one instance alone. There are 333 prophecies concerning Christ which have been fulfilled to the letter. By the law of probability, there is only one chance in eighty-three billion that 333 prophecies could be fulfilled in one person. How do we account for the accuracy and dependability of the Old Testament prophecies concerning Christ? The answer is the Holy Spirit (see Acts 1:16).

2. Divinely Indited

"Holy men of God spoke as they were moved by the Holy Spirit" (2 Pet. 1:21).

Such men were impelled by the power of the Holy Spirit, above and beyond their times, so that they were able to see, hear, and record things quite outside the realm of human imagination. Under such control, fallible men became infallible and faultless in the act of speaking or writing—sometimes even unconsciously, as in the case of Caiaphas when he prophesied of the death of Christ (see John 11:49–52), or Balaam, when he blessed the children of Israel instead of cursing them (see Num. 23–24).

3. Divinely Imprinted

"Beginning at Moses and all the Prophets, He expounded to them in all the Scriptures the things concerning Himself" (Lk. 24:27). The Bible was not only inspired by God the Father, indited by God the Holy Spirit, but also imprinted by God the Son. He put His stamp of authority not only on the Old Testament Scriptures, but also on the New Testament record that was yet to be written. St. Augustine once said: "Jesus is latent in the Old Testament, and patent in the New." Christ set His imprint on every page (see John 5:39, John 14:16, John 16:13). Therefore, we cannot accept less of that which He inspires, indites, and imprints.

B. God's Infallible Rule for Men

"The word of the Lord" (1 Pet. 1:25). Many think that the Bible should be an authority on every subject, but this is essentially wrong. The Bible was never intended to teach knowledge which men, by patient labor, may obtain for themselves. For example, the Bible was never intended to be an authority of science. Even so, Sir Charles Marston categorically asserted that "there are no contradictions between facts stated in the Scriptures and facts that have been ascertained and brought to light in any department of literature and scientific research." The Bible was never intended to be an authority on philosophy, though the wonderful book contains sound philosophy. Moreover, the Bible was never intended to be an authority on history, though no other book gives such an accurate record of human history and the true character of the heart of man. In the last analysis, the Bible was intended to be an infallible record to men and an infallible rule for men in matters of faith and practice. For this reason, the church has acknowledged the supreme authority of the Bible as God's written Word, as the deposit of the message of salvation, as the "only rule of faith and obedience, teaching what man is to believe concerning God, and what duty God requires of man."* Paul sums this up in his great statement in 2 Timothy 3:16–17: "All Scripture is given by inspiration of God, and is profitable for doctrine, for reproof, for correction, for instruction in

_____

* *The Larger Catechism*, questions 3 and 5.

righteousness, that the man of God may be complete, thoroughly equipped for every good work." In the light of this, we may state confidently that the Bible is infallible; it is "the word of the Lord" (1 Pet. 1:25).

> *Dr. Robert D. Wilson, former professor of Semitic philology at Princeton Theological Seminary, said, "After . . . years of scholarly research in Biblical textual studies and in language study, I have come to the conviction that no man knows enough to assail the truthfulness of the Old Testament. Where there is sufficient documentary evidence to make an investigation, the statements of the Bible, in the original text, have stood the test."*

II. The Indestructibility of the Bible

"The word of the Lord endures forever" (1 Pet. 1:25). The Bible is indestructible in that it outlives its foes. Jesus said, "Heaven and earth will pass away, but My words will by no means pass away" (Matt. 24:35); and again, "The Scripture cannot be broken" (John 10:35). To believe in the indestructibility of the Bible we need to consider something of the story of:

A. Its Preservation

The Bible contains the oldest books in the world. The first portions were written over 3,000 years ago—nearly a thousand years earlier than any other history we have. Herodotus, one of the oldest whose writings are with us today, was contemporary with Ezra and Nehemiah, the last of the historians of the Old Testament. Between these and Moses there was an interval of nearly a thousand years. Throughout its long history, the Bible has been burned, hidden, criticized, ridiculed, and neglected; yet God has preserved it.

> *Infidels have been at work for centuries, firing away at the Bible and making as much impression as you would shooting boiled peas at the Rock of Gibraltar! Voltaire, toward the end of his life, declared that his writings would displace the Bible, and that in 100 years the Word of God would be forgotten. In twenty-five years, the publishing house which propagated Voltaire's works became the center of the Geneva Bible Society, and the ninety beautifully-bound volumes written against the*

*Bible were sold for pennies apiece. About the same time, one
very old copy of an Old Testament manuscript was sold for
thousands of dollars. Truly, the word of the Lord endures forever.*

B. Its Publication

The Bible is never off the printing press. At least one book in
the Bible has been translated into over 2,200 languages, the complete
Bible into more than 370 languages, and the complete New
Testament into more than 950 languages. For years past, Bibles and
New Testaments have sold at the rate of thirty million copies a year;
this is, fifty every minute. It is by far the world's best seller. As
missionary literature, the Bible has reached more nations, tribes and
people than any other book in the world. Missionaries have gone to
people with no written language, have caught the significance of
words, built an alphabet and grammar, and put the Bible into that
language. This has been done over 300 times. These statistics are
constantly changing because of the miracle of publication. God has
promised to prosper His Word (see Isa. 55:11).

*A century ago, Robert J. Thomas, a Welshman working with
the Scottish Bible Society, yearned to take Bibles to Korea. His
knowledge of the language taught him that Korean is based on
Chinese, and that the educated Koreans could read it. He
boarded an American ship, but a battle broke out between the
ship's officers and the Korean Coast Guard. The ship was
destroyed and all passengers lost. Before his death, Thomas
managed to stagger out of the water carrying Bibles for
Koreans, who clubbed him to death. Today? Korea has a larger
Christian population than any other Far Eastern country.*

III. The Indispensability of the Bible

This is the word of good tidings which was preached unto you"
(1 Pet. 1:25, RV). We can do without many books, but we cannot
dispense with the Bible. It contains the only word of the gospel for
men and women. Within its covers we have an authoritative
statement concerning:

A. *The Revelation of God*

"God, who at various times and in different ways spoke in time past to the fathers by the prophets" (Heb. 1:1). While Christ is the final and authoritative revelation of God, the Bible is the final and authoritative revelation of Christ. John brings these two thoughts together in the first and twentieth chapters of his Gospel. Speaking of Christ as the revelation of God, he says, "No one has seen God at any time. The only begotten Son, who is in the bosom of the Father, He has declared [or expounded] Him" (John 1:18); and again: "These [signs] are written that you may believe that Jesus is the Christ, the Son of God, and that believing you may have life in His name" (John 20:31). Christ is central to the book. Every page of Holy Scripture focuses on Him. To encounter Christ is to look into the very face of God, for in the Lord Jesus we have "the brightness of His glory and the express image of His person" (Heb. 1:3). Yes, we can observe the majesty, divinity, and authority of God in creation, but we know nothing of His personal love, mercy, and grace until we meet Jesus Christ.

B. *The Redemption of Man*

"This is the word of good tidings which was preached unto you" (1 Pet. 1:25, RV). Man needs redeeming, but where does one find the plan of redemption? Search the philosophies of man and the religions of the world, but you search in vain. The Bible says, "Nor is there salvation in any other, for there is no other name under heaven given among men by which we must be saved" (Acts 4:12). John Wesley once wrote: " I am a creature of a day, passing through life as an arrow through the air. I am a spirit, coming from God, and returning to God. . . . I want to know one thing—the way to heaven. God Himself has condescended to teach that way. He has written it down in a book. O give me that book! At any price, give me the book of God!" In the sweep of redemption, the Bible is indispensable to:

1. *Personal Salvation*

Writing to young Timothy, Paul reminds him that from childhood he had known the Holy Scriptures. This is the only book able to make a person wise unto salvation through faith in Christ Jesus (see

2 Tim. 3:15). No wonder the Chinese man who had read through
the Bible several times admitted, "Whoever made this book made
me."

2. Social Integration

Writing to husbands and wives, parents and children, masters
and servants, Paul says, "Let the word of Christ dwell in you richly
in all wisdom" (Col. 3:16). Only then would husbands love their
wives, wives submit to their husbands, children obey their parents,
parents provoke not their children to wrath, servants obey their
masters and do all things heartily as to the Lord. The sanctity of
married life, the security of family life, and the stability of social
life are linked to the moral and ethical codes taught in the Old and
New Testaments.

3. National Reformation

"Righteousness exalts a nation, but sin is a reproach to any
people" (Prov. 14:34). The Bible is the only authority on the kind of
righteousness that exalts a nation. No other book has to its credit
such a record of lives redeemed, moral outcasts regenerated,
distressed and anxious souls cheered, and individuals and nations
remade. Never has the world known a higher code of ethics. Nor
has any other book ever so influenced for good literature, language,
art, music, and education. Personal, social and national prosperity
can only come through the preaching of the Word of God.

> *Bruce Buursma, Religion editor of the* Chicago Tribune
> Press Service, *did a write-up entitled "Bible Cure for U.S.:
> Meese" which appeared in the March 4, 1982, issue of the paper.
> In it he said: "Presidential Counselor Edwin Meese, a layman
> in the Lutheran Church-Missouri Synod, told a gathering of
> conservative Christians here [San Diego] . . . that the Bible
> holds the answers to the nation's problems. Speaking at the
> start of a four-day Congress on the Bible, Meese said: 'Nothing
> is more important in this nation today than this conference on
> the Bible—not unemployment, not rebuilding our defense
> capabilities. What is important is rebuilding our relationship
> to God and a right view of the Bible.' He said: 'There is in our
> nation a general poverty of the soul. Too many of our people*

*have taken too many wrong roads. We need a reliable road map, and that road map is the Bible.' Meese said President Reagan applauds the involvement of 'Bible-believing Christians' in public policy debates."**

If we accept our text, then we must believe the Bible is infallible and learn it; we must believe the Bible is indestructible and love it; we must believe the Bible is indispensable and live it.

Dr. Olford is Founder and Senior Lecturer at the Stephen Olford Center for Biblical Preaching in Memphis, Tennessee.

---

* Copyrighted 1982, *Chicago Tribune*, all rights reserved.

Dr. Dorothy Kelley Patterson

General Editor of The Woman's Study Bible

A Scholarly Christian Woman Looks at the Bible

Why the Bible, God's Word, Is Important to Women

Affirmation of Worth

The world has been flooded with great literature throughout history, and much of it has come from the pens of women. Instruction, entertainment and inspiration come from the printed page. However, no literature has ever compared to the blessed Holy Book which comes from the heart of God Himself. The Bible is the only book with the power to save because it presents the *one way* to God.

In the Bible the Creator presented His perfect plan, and upon its pages a woman finds her purpose and place in God's world. Though Satan used a woman to bring sin into the world, God chose a woman through whom to give the Savior who would provide redemption. As a woman, I am created in His image and redeemed by His death on the cross, and I rejoice in my salvation!

My godly parents used the Word of God to introduce me to the Father and His love. Sermons can be preached and testimonies offered; inspirational words can be penned and Christ-honoring songs can be sung. But ultimately all that we know about God, including His plan for redemption, comes to us through the pages of Scripture. My opportunity to become a "daughter of the king" and thus a "child of God" is explained and affirmed in the Bible. All that I know about Jesus and redemption is found in the Bible. If for no other reason, the Bible is precious to me because it presents my Savior and opens for me the road to heaven. *His/story* of redemption can become for every woman *her/story* of deliverance (see *The Woman's Study Bible,** p. viii).

---

* Dorothy Kelley Patterson, General Editor (Nashville, TN: Thomas Nelson, 1995).

Instruction for Living

The Bible instructs me in the ways of the Lord. Biblical principles have taught me a Christ-honoring lifestyle. As a woman, I have sought and found intellectual challenge and moral standard, as well as spiritual refreshment, on the pages of God's Holy Word.

The Bible is the one reliable standard, the supreme guide, the only inerrant and infallible authority, and the sole criterion by which I can judge matters of faith and conduct. When I come to Scripture, I move beyond the need to choose my own way or determine my own path. I know that God's Word does not merely contain truth, it *is* truth, and God's Word cannot lead me astray. The Bible offers comfort and hope to the suffering and dying; its wisdom is of incalculable worth. To unlock God's Word is to share His promises and accept His challenges.

Throughout history women have affirmed the importance of Scripture in their lives. For example, Queen Elizabeth I of England said, "I walk many times . . . into the pleasant fields of the Holy Scriptures, where I pluck up the goodly green herbs of sentences, eat them by reading, chew them up musing, and lay them up at length in the seat of memory . . . so that I may the less perceive the bitterness of this life." Queen Victoria, another British monarch, once presented a Bible to an African prince, saying, "Here is the secret of England's greatness."

Helen Keller—deaf, mute and blind—often referred to her Braille Bible as her most valued possession. Jenny Lind, the world-renowned opera star, once wrote to a friend, "My Bible was never more precious to me than now, never more truly my stay. I drink there in rest, self-knowledge, hope, faith, love, carefulness, and the fear of God. Would that all men would come to this knowledge and that we all daily feasted on this divine Book."

Margaret Thatcher, a former Prime Minister of Great Britain, alluded to her strict Methodist upbringing, referring often to the Old and New Testaments and affirming that she had been brought up "to honor all of the fundamental beliefs of the Christian church."

My own testimony affirms that of these women. I have found that the Bible keeps me on the right path. When I completed my seminary experience and moved, with my husband and two babies, to Fayetteville, Arkansas, I was torn between the overwhelming responsibilities of being the wife of a busy pastor and the mother of an infant and preschooler on the one hand and, on the other hand, of using the training and giftedness I had acquired through sacrificial investment of my time and energy (as well as my husband's financial resources) in theological education. I expected to do great things for God in the church and the kingdom; I assumed that I would use my thorough foundation in Biblical studies, my translation skills in Greek and Hebrew, and my practical equipping for preparing and delivering messages to change the lives of women through teaching the Bible. However, that congregation already had a resident premier Bible teacher, and that expected ministry simply did not materialize. In addition, the responsibilities of my home and family demanded far more than what I had expected in time and energy. Seminary had not addressed the issue facing me: I was a woman supposedly gifted in Biblical exposition (a rare commodity in the evangelical world of the '60s) whose platform was a parsonage demanding maintenance and whose audience consisted of babbling babies, and my heart was asking, "Just how are you going to use all that seminary training?"

At this point in my own personal pilgrimage, I was driven to the Word. I remember, day after day, locking myself in the bathroom while the children were napping in order to resume the devotional reading of God's Word—a practice that had been subsumed during seminary days by my diligent translation of the text and study of the Scripture. Suddenly I was out of the academy and in the wilderness. The erudition and polish acquired in seminary seemed to have no place in my real-world drama, and the spiritual sustenance for which my heart and spirit cried were strangely absent.

In the wilderness of going about the mundane tasks of a homemaker, the delicacies of textual criticism, church history, Christian ethics, missiology, homiletics, philosophy of religion, and Greek and Hebrew exegesis were missing; but the manna was there! However, I became painfully aware that yesterday's manna would not meet today's needs. Just as the children of Israel were instructed to gather manna day by day, I must seize my spiritual manna on a daily basis.

Beginning in Genesis and continuing systematically through the whole of Scripture, I read a daily portion—no commentaries or extra-Biblical sources—just His Word. I rediscovered the nutrients in God's pure Word—the nourishment that comes from simply reading His Word for personal edification, not to prepare for testing or performance but simply to meet my own heart's need. I always began my reading with this prayer question, "What does the Bible have to say to me about what I am supposed to be and do?" This experience changed my life and focus. Years later, from the discipline of that wilderness experience came a series of messages for women under the byline "The Bible Speaks on Being a Woman."

In my own life, I came to realize that my choice to marry and bear children brought some boundaries that would affect forever my ministry in the kingdom. I learned that the keeping of my home, the helping my husband, and the rearing of our children were all ministries unto the Lord that would take priority over any other kingdom ministries. As I began to pour my time and energies into these primary responsibilities, I began to amass wisdom that only comes from saturation in God's Word and from experiences in life that flesh out the Biblical principles. I had opportunity to put into practice in my own life the principles I would later be teaching women in local churches and in the seminary classroom. What seemed to be rejection and a closed door was actually God's redirection to an open door: to challenge women to live their lives according to Biblical principles.

My education and training had uniquely equipped me to explain the Scripture; my life as a wife and mother and committed homemaker provided the vehicle to show that the Biblical principles could be manifested in a life poured into home and family, yet augmented by kingdom service to Christ according to the seasons of life through which every woman passes. I went through almost two decades of not using my skills and training except for my own personal edification, but now I find myself at the heart of a program in women's studies which helps my seminary president husband by equipping women for ministry in the theological community.

My priorities have not changed, but the way those priorities are manifested has evolved through the years under the leadership of my husband. It was he who insisted that I pursue theological education, including graduate and post-graduate degree programs; it was he who enabled me to put all of that aside and pour my life into my home and children; it was he who continued to encourage me.to be a part of his life and ministry; it was he who called me out of "retirement" to develop the curriculum and pilot the courses in the MDiv in Women's Studies for Southeastern Baptist Theological Seminary. However, before my husband could lead me into this life of fulfilling ministry and joyous service, I had to wrestle with the demands of Scripture and determine to let God's Word be my final authority on priorities and lifestyle.

If I have made or will make any contribution to the kingdom of Christ, that contribution will be traced back to the role of Scripture in my own life. Without a Word from God, I would not have had the courage to put aside personal desires and ambition, nor would I have had the discernment to determine where to put my time and energies. Many times my own logic and personal whims would have taken me a different way. I was held to the path only by a commitment to obedience to Scripture and sustained in that journey by my faith in His faithfulness.

A Reminder

In a sense, a woman is uniquely in tune with the sanctity of life (and conversely with the finality of death) because of the maternity that is interwoven into her very nature. Eve was described as "the mother of all living." Women throughout the Old Testament struggled with the burden of barrenness and considered infertility to be the worst of all afflictions. The sanctity of life seems to be uniquely embedded into the very nature of a woman. Even in this modern era, any woman who bears a child in some sense puts her own life on the line. The regulations for covenant living recorded in Deuteronomy contain an obscure reference to the unique bonding of a mother and her offspring: "You shall not boil a young goat in its mother's milk" (Deut. 14:21). In this reference, the milk, which would usually be a means of sustaining life, would become the means of death. Perhaps this admonition was a warning to those who would look contemptuously on the relationship between a mother and her offspring. In my own experience, I remember vividly my first pregnancy, which occurred while I was still in the university. My first thought was surprise that God's timing was not any better! I was in my first year of Greek and still struggling to complete my baccalaureate degree. It would have been easier to wait until that initial degree was complete before trying to balance family and education. But then I began to miscarry, and suddenly I was overwhelmed by the brief journey between life and death. To deal with my anxieties and questions I turned again to God's Word. I was reminded that He alone controls life and death—whether my baby lived or died was in His hands. During the months that followed, my baby died. I had the burden of my own initial indifference to the pregnancy, the sorrow of the loss of my own flesh and blood, the physical and emotional pain of a traumatic miscarriage. Where could I turn for comfort and healing?—God's Word. Scripture was faithful to provide all I needed then, whether correction for a wrong attitude or comfort for a hurting heart, and it will be faithful to provide all I will need in the future.

Conclusion

The Bible is the foundation for my faith journey. Its precepts were emblazoned on my heart by godly parents, who introduced me to the Christ revealed on its pages. Now its words strengthen, comfort, teach, and edify me. I not only see my worth as a woman in His image, but I also have learned the importance of my unique feminine role assignment to be a helper to my husband and nurturer to my children.

In 1895, Elizabeth Cady Stanton published *The Woman's Bible*.* She alleged that the Bible was oppressive to women and thus placed herself over Scripture, making her own personal experience the ultimate standard for interpreting Scripture. However, there is another option for women. I invite women to join me in choosing to

* Not to be confused with *The Woman's Study Bible*, referred to on page 150.

line up under the authority of Scripture, seeking to understand the message of the Bible and committing themselves to live out its principles in faith and practice. Sometimes that means a woman must dig more deeply into Scripture to find a word from God. Scripture must not be twisted or rewritten, nor can words be redefined, nor can one choose what is or is not authoritative. In making the decisions of life, a woman must faithfully seek a word from God and then commit herself to be obedient in doing what He says.

"The inexhaustible Word of God will introduce you [every woman] to the Father and His love; it will unveil and give understanding of His will; it will reveal His Law and principles for living; it will offer intellectual challenges for your mind, moral values for your will, and spiritual refreshment for your heart" (*The Woman's Study Bible*, p. viii).

Dr. Thomas D. Elliff

A Southern Baptist Pastoral Leader Looks at the Bible

You have asked me to share why I believe the Bible is God's Word and, therefore, true and to be trusted. My reply arises from a deep sense of reverence. Admittedly, my answers are subjective, for that is the nature of your question. They will not satisfy some, nor are they intended to be an apologetic for the Scripture. As you will soon see, I believe the Bible does not so much need *defense* as it needs *declaration*. With that understanding, I will set about to answer your question.

1. I believe the Bible is true in the EMPIRICAL sense. Over the centuries the "facts" in the Scripture have been subjected to constant attack. They have been the subject of criticism and scrutiny. Yet, as one has said, the Bible is like an anvil, wearing out hammer after hammer of criticism. When put to the test of true and honest scholarship, all its apparent contradictions are dispelled. The "challenging statements" in the Bible are only *certified* under the microscope of a fair examination.

2. I believe the Bible is true in the EMOTIONAL sense. I make no apology for this statement, since I have been asked to reveal my heart. I grew up with a predisposition to the Bible as the true Word of God. Those who scoff at my prejudice are possessed of theirs as well. They are predisposed to believe that truth can be found in some other source or manner. Interestingly, most who scoff at the Scripture believe that truth is resident in *themselves*. Encouraged by godly parents and friends I, however, grew up believing that there was higher, more noble truth than that which emanated from my own imagination—and that this truth is in the Word of God.

3. I believe the Bible is true in the EFFECTIVE sense. People

who subscribe to the veracity and authority of the Scripture and bring themselves under that authority seem guided along more noble paths than others. Yes, there are hypocrites who have used the Bible falsely to support their own mean and wicked agendas. History has proven, however, that the problem is not in the nature of the Scripture but in their own wicked hearts. Bible-believing people seem more charitable, with greater reverence for life, than those who reject God's Word.

4. I believe the Bible is true in the EXPERIENTIAL sense. In my own experience I have found the principles of God's Word to be immutable. My own life has been subject to blessing or discipline as a result of obedience or violation of those principles.

5. I believe the Bible is true in the sense of the ENCOUR-AGEMENT I receive from the Spirit of God when reading it. This highly subjective "heart affirmation" is present as I read the Bible. The very reading of it challenges my faith and changes my life. Books which oppose or contradict the Bible, however, do not provide the same spiritual endorsement. Nor do they lift my faith to God.

6. I believe the Bible is true in the ELEMENTAL sense. I find that whether I am considering the Bible as a whole or in its various parts, I can do nothing to improve on the Bible or to make it more true. It is "true truth" throughout.

7. I believe the Bible is true in the sense of the ENDORSEMENT it has received through the centuries by those who have given it serious study and sought to apply it in their own lives. I find that the people of history I hold in highest esteem are overwhelmingly those who have affirmed the Bible as true. Additionally, Christ Himself affirmed the veracity of the Scriptures, as did the human writers of both the Old and New Testaments. The Bible is endorsed in both the earthly and heavenly realms.

8. I believe the Bible is true in the sense of the ENLIGHT-ENMENT it brings to my own heart as I read it. When I read the Bible my "eyes are opened" and I begin to see things as they really are. The Bible moves me past pretense, right to the heart of every matter. It reveals my own heart—sometimes embarrassingly so. I

cannot argue with its verdict for I know it is accurate.

9. I believe the Bible is true in the ENDURING sense. When the Psalmist cried, "Forever, O Lord, thy word is settled in heaven" (Psalm 119:89), he was saying that the Bible is truth for the ages. It is neither more nor less true with the discoveries or exigencies of each passing generation.

10. I believe the Bible is true in its ENTIRETY. I do not find some parts more true or inspired than others. Over the years I have discovered that some portions I may have earlier considered unnecessary, uninteresting, or inconsequential have later become great and significant sources of light.

11. I believe the Bible is true in the ENABLING sense. When I proceed according to the Word of God there is effectiveness and accomplishment. But when I proceed on my own and in a way contrary to the clear leading of the Scriptures, I have met repeated discouragement and failure.

12. I believe the Bible is true in the sense of ENDUEMENT from on high. It is increasingly apparent to me that the mere speaking of the Word of God is attended with greater effect in both the earthly and spiritual realm than anything I can utter out of my own heart.

Finally—for we all must face God in eternity—consider this experience that millions could corroborate: I have often attended the bedside of both dying saints and sinners. Never in all the years of my experience have I been asked to bend close so that I might hear a dying man *renounce* the Word of God. But often I have been asked by those who were looking eternity in the face: "*Read to me, please, from the Bible.*" Why do they register that request? Because death brings with it thoughts of many uncertainties. It is in that moment a man wants most to hear what his own heart tells him are the *certainties* of God.

Yes, without question, I believe the Bible is truth—God's truth—and without any mixture of error.

Dr. Elliff is the pastor of First Southern Baptist Church, Del City, OK and Past President of the Southern Baptist Convention.

Appendix

Names the Bible Uses for Itself that Indicate Its Validity

In context, some of these passages have reference to a particular portion of the Bible, while others are speaking more generally. All are quoted from the King James Version.

Isaiah 34:16
> Seek ye out of **the book of the LORD**, and read. . . .

Nehemiah 8:3
> And he read therein . . . and the ears of all the people were attentive unto **the book of the law**.

Hebrews 6:5
> And have tasted **the good word of God**, and the powers of the world to come.

Romans 1:2
> Which he had promised afore by his prophets in **the holy scriptures**.

2 Timothy 3:15
> And that from a child thou hast known **the holy scriptures**, which are able to make thee wise unto salvation through faith which is in Christ Jesus.

Psalm 1:2
> But his delight is in **the law of the LORD**; and in his law doth he meditate day and night.

Isaiah 30:9
> That this is a rebellious people, lying children, children that will not hear **the law of the LORD**.

Romans 3:2
> Much every way: chiefly, because that unto them were committed **the oracles of God**.

Luke 11:28
> But he said, Yea rather, blessed are they that hear **the word of God**, and keep it.

Hebrews 4:12

For **the word of God** is quick, and powerful, and sharper than any twoedged sword, piercing even to the dividing asunder of soul and spirit, and of the joints and marrow, and is a discerner of the thoughts and intents of the heart.

Colossians 3:16

Let **the word of Christ** dwell in you richly in all wisdom; teaching and admonishing one another in psalms and hymns and spiritual songs, singing with grace in your hearts to the Lord.

Philippians 2:16

Holding forth **the word of life**; that I may rejoice in the day of Christ, that I have not run in vain, neither laboured in vain.

2 Timothy 2:15

Study to shew thyself approved unto God, a workman that needeth not to be ashamed, rightly dividing **the word of truth**.

James 1:18

Of his own will begat he us with **the word of truth**, that we should be a kind of firstfruits of his creatures.

Ezekiel 6:3

And say, Ye mountains of Israel, hear **the word of the Lord GOD**; Thus saith the Lord GOD to the mountains, and to the hills, to the rivers, and to the valleys; Behold, I, even I, will bring a sword upon you, and I will destroy your high places.

Acts 13:48

And when the Gentiles heard this, they were glad, and glorified **the word of the Lord**: and as many as were ordained to eternal life believed.

Acts 19:10

And this continued by the space of two years; so that all they which dwelt in Asia heard **the word of the Lord Jesus**, both Jews and Greeks.

1 Thessalonians 1:8

For from you sounded out **the word of the Lord** not only in Macedonia and Achaia, but also in every place your faith to Godward is spread abroad; so that we need not to speak any thing.

Dr. Robert Gee Witty

Robert Gee Witty, having experienced "rebirth" as a child, received a call to the ministry as a teenager.

His educational training included a liberal university, both Wesleyan and Calvinistic seminaries, and culminated in the Ph. D. program in Classical Rhetoric at the University of Florida.

After pastoral experience of two-score years in the Southern Baptist Convention, he founded the Luther Rice Seminary, Jacksonville, Florida, and served as President for twenty years with an international ministry.

He is the author of several books published by the Broadman Press. In addition to a radio and internet ministry, he presently serves as a semiretired Bible teacher, church consultant, and writer.